WITHDRAWN
UTSA LIBRARIES

P9-DTS-183

THE MENTALLY ILL IN JAIL

THE GUILFORD LAW AND BEHAVIOR SERIES
John Monahan, Loren H. Roth, and
Stephen J. Morse, Editors

THE MENTALLY ILL IN JAIL
Planning for Essential Services
Henry J. Steadman, Dennis W. McCarty,
and Joseph P. Morrisey

REFORMING THE LAW
Impact of Child Development Research
Gary B. Melton, Editor

PSYCHOLOGICAL EVALUATIONS FOR THE COURTS
A Handbook for Mental Health Professionals and Lawyers
Gary B. Melton, John Petrila, Norman G. Poythress, and
Christopher Slobogin

INFORMED CONSENT
A Study of Decisionmaking in Psychiatry
Charles W. Lidz, Alan Meisel, Eviatar Zerubavel, Mary Carter,
Regina M. Sestak, and Loren H. Roth

THE MENTALLY ILL IN JAIL
Planning for Essential Services

Henry J. Steadman
Dennis W. McCarty
Joseph P. Morrissey

The Guilford Press
New York   London

© 1989 The Guilford Press
A Division of Guilford Publications, Inc.
72 Spring Street, New York, NY 10012

All rights reserved

No part of this book may be reproduced, stored in a retrieval system,
or transmitted, in any form or by any means, electronic, mechanical,
photocopying, microfilming, recording, or otherwise, without written
permission from the Publisher.

Printed in the United States of America

Last digit is print number: 9 8 7 6 5 4 3 2 1

Library of Congress Cataloging-in-Publication Data

Steadman, Henry J.
    The mentally ill in jail : planning for essential services
 / Henry J. Steadman, Dennis W. McCarty, and Joseph P. Morrissey.
     p. cm. (The Guilford law and behavior series)
    Bibliography: p.
    Includes index.
    ISBN 0-89862-279-4
    1. Prisoners—Psychiatric care. 2. Insane, Criminal and
dangerous—Mental health services. I. McCarty, Dennis W.
II. Morrissey, Joseph P. III. Title. IV. Series
RC451.4.P68S72 1989
365'.66—dc19   88-24157
                                   CIP

Library
University of Texas
at San Antonio

To Saleem Shah

A true friend and valued colleague to whom the field of law and mental health owes a great debt.

Preface

The dominant approach to the problems of the mentally ill in local jails seems to be that of blaming someone else. Correctional staffs and the press tend to blame the mental health system for deinstitutionalizing state mental hospitals; as these groups see it, unprepared and mentally ill patients are dumped into the streets, only to be arrested and to produce severe problems in jail. Mental health professionals, for their part, blame law enforcement agents for unnecessarily arresting persons whose only "crime" is being mentally ill. The public, in its turn, finds fault with both the mental health and criminal justice systems for exposing them to so much perceived risk from the mentally ill on city streets. We hope that our book will diminish these accusations, both by emphasizing the community-wide scope of the problem and by offering some concrete suggestions for addressing the thorny problem of the mentally ill in local jails.

When we began the research on which this book is based, it was difficult to obtain any information beyond anecdotes or single-program descriptions of mental health services for jail inmates. We attempted to broaden these descriptions by taking a systematic approach to characterizing a substantial number of jail programs in various parts of the country. More importantly, we wanted to determine whether certain ways of providing services regularly worked better than others. As the reader will see, the answer to that was no, but some basic principles emerged from those sites we studied that had the most effective planning of mental health services for jail inmates.

In developing the original research, Christopher Dunn, then of the National Institute of Mental Health's Center for the Study of Antisocial and Violent Behavior and now of Bowling Green University, and Carole Morgan-Hardy were key supporters. Chris encouraged our interest in the topic area and introduced us to the training Carole was providing under National Institute of Corrections support to jail staff. Our small-scale evaluation of Carole's training led to the larger grant application that supported this study. The jail mental health programs that participated in Carole's training sessions became the primary sample for our research.

The conduct of the research was a tribute to a tremendously dedicated, congenial, and productive project staff that ably combined fieldwork skills with analytic expertise. Hal Kilburn, Nancy Eliot Sampson, and C. Lee Scott-Mack provided a continuity of effort that made the research as enjoyable as it was productive. Michael Lindsey and Pamela Clark Robbins also made significant contributions during the data analysis phase of the project.

In the jails themselves, the security, administrative, and mental health staffs without exception were willing to allow us into their facilities and to give us their valuable time. They were concerned with the seriousness of the issues they faced and were anxious to help us understand what they were doing, what they thought should be done, and the constraints they faced.

To fill out the material from the research project, we asked for chapters from Richard Warner, Joel Dvoskin, and Judith Cox, Gerald Landsberg, and M. Peter Paravati. All agreed to write chapters demonstrating how the program with which they were involved exemplified the planning principles that emerged from our research, and they did so in a very short time.

A special acknowledgment must go to Alan Meisel and Loren H. Roth. Both very carefully read the initial draft and suggested additional material that has greatly strengthened the range of relevant material in this book.

Finally, a word of thanks is due to Theresa Flansburg, who deftly juggled multiple versions of this manuscript over the years during which it was under preparation. Not only were our drafts rapidly and efficiently turned around, but not a chapter, paragraph, or sentence was lost on a sometimes word-eating word processor. It is because of people such as her that the final product from all the other people mentioned here will see the light of day.

Henry J. Steadman
Dennis W. McCarty
Joseph P. Morrissey

Contents

I

POLICY AND PRACTICE

Chapter 1

The Jail under Siege

Administrators of local jails are in the midst of a crisis that threatens virtually the entire range of jail operations. Conditions in these facilities have always been poor for the most part, but the situation is now acute in many jurisdictions. Nearly half of the jails in the United States are over 30 years old ("New Jails," 1981). Extensive renovations are needed at many facilities just to meet minimal state standards. Some sheriffs are refusing to accept new prisoners because their jails are already operating far in excess of capacity (Carney, 1982), and public attitudes have made it difficult to obtain funding for needed services.

Exacerbating the problems of inadequate physical plants and tight funding is the explosion of the jail population. Between 1978 and 1986, the number of inmates in U.S. jails increased by 73%, from 158,394 to 274,444. This 8-year increase was three times higher than any previous 8-year increase (Bureau of Justice Statistics, 1987). Conditions are so bad that both state and federal courts are intervening to order sweeping changes in jail operations, despite the conservative judicial standard for such cases established by the U.S. Supreme Court in *Bell v. Wolfish* (1979).[1] Officials estimate that anywhere from 11%

---

1. In *Bell v. Wolfish* (1979), the Supreme Court accelerated the trend toward a presumptive validity of prior regulations and thereby assumed a "hands-off" posture with respect to most correctional practices. The Court noted that while constitutional rights must be scrupulously observed, "the inquiry of federal courts into prison management must be limited to the issue of whether a particular system violates any prohibition of the Constitution. . . . The wide range of 'judgement calls' that meet constitutional and statutory requirements are confided to officials outside of the Judicial Branch of Government" (p. 1886).

3

(Kerle & Ford, 1982) to 33% (National Association of Counties, 1982) of all jails are under a court order or consent decree as a result of constitutionally deficient procedures or programming.

Within this context, the availability of mental health services and other types of human services for inmates of local jails has become a major concern for professionals and citizens' groups over the past decade (Newman & Price, 1977a, 1977b; General Accounting Office, 1980; Morgan, 1981; Dunn & Steadman, 1982). In 1982 there were 3,300 jails in the United States, ranging from one- or two-person rural jails to metropolitan complexes with upward of 5,000 inmates (Kerle & Ford, 1982). Most jails are county or municipal facilities that operate as short-term pretrial holding units for the courts (57% in 1982; Bureau of Justice Statistics, 1983) and as detention units for offenders serving sentences of less than 1 year (43%).

In the past, given the rapid turnover of inmates and a mandate primarily for safe retention of criminals until disposition, jail authorities and county fiscal officers did not consider mental health services their responsibility. Inmates with serious psychiatric and behavioral problems were transferred to state mental hospitals, which were used as primary service providers. Other agencies were expected to deal with the mental health problems of inmates after their release to the community. Only for some of the most acutely suicidal or disturbed inmates were crisis intervention services available in the jail, usually in the form of physician-prescribed psychotropic medications. In only a few instances was the jail seen as a major provider of mental health services.

Beginning in the early 1970s, however, far-reaching reforms of the mental health, legal, and criminal justice systems markedly altered the social context surrounding jail operations (Goldfarb, 1976; Ringel & Segal, 1986). The rapid deinstitutionalization of state mental hospitals, for example, led to the relocation of thousands of mental patients to community settings (Bachrach, 1980; Bassuk & Gerson, 1978; Morrissey, 1982a). A number of reports have indicated that many of these patients were often arrested and incarcerated in local jails on misdemeanor charges as a way of dealing with their disturbed behavior (Abramson, 1972; Zitrin, Hardesty, & Burdock, 1976;

Whitmer, 1980; Lamb & Grant, 1982). Although such actions may in part have been a consequence of civil libertarian reforms that led to the imposition of much more stringent standards for involuntary commitment and to a corresponding reduction in state mental hospital beds (Robitscher, 1976), the effect of these changes was to significantly curtail admissions to state mental hospitals (Morrissey & Tessler, 1982) and to make jail transfers to these facilities much more difficult to accomplish.

The courts have also directly intervened on behalf of inmates in local jails. Class action suits in Pittsburgh, Phoenix, Las Vegas, Washington, D.C., and elsewhere have resulted in court-imposed minimum medical and mental health services (Singer, 1981; Morgan, 1981). And although it is still unclear whether these developments have led to a dramatic increase in the number of mentally disturbed inmates in local jails (Steadman & Ribner, 1980) or have simply heightened the awareness of a long-term problem, the current picture is one of burgeoning jail populations that correctional administrators perceive to have a significant need for mental health services. So, even if the proportion of inmates with mental health problems has remained constant, there has still been a dramatic increase in the absolute number of prisoners in need of professional care.

Despite these developments, there are no comprehensive national data on the scope and level of diagnosed mental health needs in local jails. However, Monahan and Steadman (1982), in a recent review of the available literature, located six studies that investigated true prevalence rates of mental disorder among jail inmates in particular jurisdictions.

1. Arthur Bolton Associates (1976) surveyed over 1,000 adult offenders in five California county jails and reported that 6.7% of the inmates were psychotic, 9.3% had a nonpsychotic mental disorder, and 21.0% had a form of "personality disorder."

2. Swank and Winer (1976) assessed 100 consecutive admissions to the Boulder County (Denver), Colorado, jail and reported that 5% were psychotic, 13% were "antisocial personalities," and 16% had "other personality disorders."

3. Schuckit, Herrmann, and Schuckit (1977) interviewed a random sample of 199 white males (whose major charges were

not drug-related) shortly after admission to the San Diego County, California, jail. Of these inmates, 3% were found to have a psychotic affective disorder and 3% to have an organic brain syndrome. "Antisocial personality" was diagnosed for 16% of the inmates, alcoholism for 15%, and drug abuse for 12%.

4. Bogira (1981) reported that 4% of the inmates in the Cook County (Chicago), Illinois, jail were classified as "psychotic, suicidal, or in a serious manic depressive or toxic state or . . . had serious adjustment problems."

5. O'Keefe (1980) studied 955 inmates in three county jails in Massachusetts and found that 4.6% of the jail admissions were sufficiently mentally ill to be committed under civil statutes by a psychiatrist, while an additional 6.2% "were noted as exhibiting signs of mental illness by jail personnel" but were not judged to be committable under criminal law.

6. The U.S. Department of Justice's 1978 Survey of Inmates of Local Jails (U.S. Department of Justice, 1980a) sampled 5,172 inmates in jails throughout the country (94% male) who were asked whether they were experiencing a "nervous disorder," a "mental problem," an "emotional problem," or "depression." Although no definition of the terms was provided, the data showed that 4.1% of the males and 6.4% of the females reported a nervous disorder, 1.6% of the males and 2.2% of the females reported an emotional problem, and 1.1% of the males and 2.4% of the females reported depression.

Of the two more recent reports on jail inmate mental health issues (Guy, Platt, Zwerling & Bullock, 1985; Meloy, 1985), the former gives actual prevalence rates. Both of these relate to large metropolitan jails—Philadelphia and San Diego, respectively.

1. Guy *et al.* (1985) chose every third admission to the Philadelphia County Prison System (which, despite the word "Prison" in its title, serves nonsentenced, recently arrested persons) over an unspecified period. The study produced 486 inmates, 96 of whom received a psychiatric diagnostic interview. The authors concluded that 11.5% were schizophrenic, 9% had personality disorders, and 12% had some other psychiatric diagnosis. In addition, 36% had some substance abuse, 5% were diagnosed as mentally retarded, and 1% had organic brain syn-

drome. Overall, they concluded that 11% of the inmates required immediate inpatient treatment and that 69% needed some type of treatment, including substance abuse treatment.

2. Meloy's (1985) report is primarily a program description of how services are provided in the psychiatric security unit of the San Diego County jail. Accordingly, true prevalence rates for the inmate population are not presented; rather, the focus is on the distribution of diagnoses of those inmates already in treatment.

These studies indicate that the true prevalence rate of severe mental disorders (i.e., psychoses) in local jails ranges from 3% to 11%, and that the rate of less severe forms of mental illness (i.e., nonpsychotic and personality disorders) varies greatly, ranging up to 15–20% (Roth, 1980). Citing community prevalence rates reported by Neugebauer, Dohrenwend, and Dohrenwend (1980), Monahan and Steadman (1982) concluded that "the weight of the evidence appears to support the assertion that the true prevalence rate of psychosis among inmate populations does not exceed the true prevalence rate of psychosis among class-matched community populations" (p. 168). Nonetheless, given the deficits of mental health services in most jails, these data also suggest that mentally ill inmates constitute a significant population in need of such services.

With the exception of a few expository reports on individual jails (e.g., Nielsen, 1979; Haley, 1980; Russel, 1980; Monahan & McDonough, 1980; Meloy, 1985) and descriptions of selected "model" programs (Morgan, 1978), the actual structure and operation of mental health services for jail inmates in the United States have not been studied. Given the paucity of any human services in most jails, it is clear that most of the almost 275,000 inmates in these facilities on any given day (Bureau of Justice Statistic, 1987) do not have access to proper mental health care (Newman & Price, 1977b; General Accounting Office, 1980; Morgan, 1981). Certainly, if current legal and mental health policy trends continue, all but the smallest jails will have to contend with the prospect of developing mental health services to safeguard the constitutional rights of their mentally ill inmates. Yet few insights are now available concerning alternative ways to deliver jail mental health services and the relative advantages and disadvantages of each approach. The research upon which this book is based was designed to address these issues.

ORIGINS AND SCOPE OF THE STUDY

Our research emerged from the Special National Workshop on Mental Health Services in Jails, which convened in Baltimore in September 1978. The workshop was organized and jointly sponsored by three federal agencies: the National Institute of Mental Health (NIMH), the National Institute of Corrections (NIC), and the National Institute of Law Enforcement and Criminal Justice (now the National Institute of Justice). The purposes of the workshop were to define problems and needs, to facilitate the exchange of information between correctional and mental health officials, to develop ideas for programs, and to provide a framework for changing mental health services in the local jails. Approximately 60 people attended. Delegates included practitioners actually working in jails, legal experts, academicians, and representatives from several administrative agencies.

One outgrowth of this conference was the recommendation that regional follow-up meetings be held in order to build on the interest in program development strategies that had been expressed there. The NIC sponsored three additional workshops in October and December 1979, organized by Carole Morgan-Hardy of Training Associates, Inc. The workshops were conducted in Hyannis, Massachusetts, Atlanta, Georgia, and Boulder, Colorado. They had three principal objectives: (1) to increase the level of awareness of those individuals directly responsible for service delivery at each of the participating locations; (2) to achieve a mutual sense of responsibility and commitment for increased program development; and (3) to devise a strategy for each location to further the development of the provision of mental health care in jails. Organizers of the 3-day workshops sought participant teams from all areas of the country that expressed a desire to upgrade jail mental health services.

The teams were to consist of three to four individuals, including key decision makers from jails and mental health systems, as well as others who were in a position to assist in the implementation strategy for each location.

Shortly after the workshops were concluded, we obtained a grant from NIMH to study the relationships between the jails that were represented at the workshops and their local mental health systems. The research was intended to delineate, among other things, the range of approaches that these jails followed in developing inmate mental health services; the availability and extent of connections with existing community mental health services; the relative effectiveness of the various program approaches; and the factors that influenced program development over a 2-year period following the initiation of the study.

Study Sample

The sample chosen for our study included the 33 jails that had been represented at the NIC training workshops. The administrators of these facilities were presumed to be very concerned with mental health programming and had experimented with a variety of service options. Ten other jails were also included in the study; these were selected either because of their reputations as having model programs or because the courts had recently ordered extensive improvements in existing services. No site had to be eliminated from the proposed sample because of refusals by jail or mental health officials to participate in our research.

The jails were located in 42 communities in 26 states. Nationally, over 75% of all jails are clustered in the southern and north central states (U.S. Department of Justice, 1981). The sample jails, by contrast, were drawn about equally from each of the four major regions of the country. Jails in the Northeast have been overrepresented and those in the South underrepresented.

The relationship between the size of all U.S. jails and the size of those in our study sample is a bit more complex. Most jails in the United States are very small. Nearly half of all local adult correctional facilities hold fewer than 10 inmates, and Miller (1978) reports that 75% hold fewer than 20. Collectively, however, the small jails hold very few inmates; most locally detained individuals are incarcerated in large urban jails. The 130 jails with populations in excess of 250 represent only 4% of all jails but hold nearly half (45%) of the men and women in custody. Except for one jail system with an average daily population of 1,575, the jail population in the sample ranged in size from 15 to 630. Although the sample thus contained a disproportionate number of medium-sized and large facilities, such facilities hold more than 70% of all inmates in U.S. jails (Goldkamp, 1978, p. 24).

Though selected on the basis of different criteria, the workshop and supplemental sites were comparable in both jail size and geographic spread. At the time at which data were collected, the workshop jails had an average daily population of 222 inmates. With the exception of one especially large jail, the average daily population of the comparison jails was 206. The 33 workshop sites were located in 21 states, while the 10 additional sites were from 9 states. (A list of the participating jails can be found in the Appendix.)

Data Collection

Each of the 42 sites was visited for 2–3 days by a two-person team that used a semistructured interview schedule to obtain information about services provided to mentally ill inmates and liaisons with community mental health service providers. Descriptions of on-site mental health programs were obtained from the mental health program chief at each jail, or from the sheriff where there was no program chief. Interviews lasted about 1 hour and focused on the volume and structure of services in eight specific areas representing a full range of mental health services: intake screening; evaluations; distribution of psychotropic medication; psychological therapy; competency examinations; drug and alcohol counseling; internal and/or external hospitalization of the acutely mentally ill; and case management at release. Key persons in the external agencies that provided mental health services to the jail, such as community mental health centers and the forensic units at state mental hospitals, were also interviewed concerning the services they provided.

Following the site visits, a questionnaire was mailed to persons we identified during those visits as being familiar with the jail mental health program. The questions concerned the perceived effectiveness of the jail mental health program and the extent of conflict among participating agencies in each county. Together, the information from on-site interviews and the perceived-effectiveness questionnaire provided a way of characterizing study sites at the outset of our research.

The third major data collection activity involved a telephone survey of all 43 sites to determine what program changes had occurred in the 12–18 months following our initial site visits. This survey involved representatives from the sheriff's department or jail administrative staff at each site, as well as one or more informants from external mental health agencies (where relevant). The content of these interviews focused on any changes in the jail's mental health services program; personnel turnover; the initiation of any litigation; budgetary changes; and any developments in the local community mental health system that had impinged on inmate mental health services.

The fourth data collection task involved a resurvey of correctional and mental health staff at each site who had responded to the original perceived-effectiveness questionnaire. The new data were collected in a questionnaire mailed in November 1982. This second questionnaire focused on the frequency and scope of day-to-day conflicts between correctional and mental health personnel in each jail's mental health program.

The final set of data was generated from 1-day site visits to three jails in January 1984. These included one of the most comprehensive jail programs we found among the 33 NIC training conference jails, and one of the most rapidly developing jail mental health programs among the 10 comparison sites. The third jail was not one of the 43 sample sites; this jail served as an NIC regional resource center and was one of the sites where our second questionnaire had been pilot-tested. These site visits provided us with the opportunity to present our findings and recommendations to knowledgeable correctional and mental health staff. The feedback we received played an important role in the formulation of the principles for program planning that are presented in Chapter 7 of this book.

OVERVIEW OF STUDY GOALS

From the outset of our research, we were struck by the virtual absence of any empirically grounded guidelines for establishing appropriate services for mentally disturbed inmates in jails and local correctional facilities. From all indications in the media and professional journals, the problem of the mentally ill in jails was intensifying because of changes in the legal, political, and economic environment of the mental health and criminal justice systems. County officials and citizens' groups throughout the country, stimulated in part by the threat of court intervention, were confronted with the myriad problems of instituting or improving mental health services for jail inmates. We recognized that a careful and systematic approach to the design and implementation of such service programs would benefit from a thorough assessment of the true prevalence of mental illness in a large, representative sample of U.S. jails. However, we also knew that epidemiological investigations of this scope and complexity would be extremely costly, difficult to implement, and of such long duration that practical implications for program design would not be immediately forthcoming. Clearly, local officials and service providers could not afford the luxury of deferring service interventions until long-term research findings became available. Rather, if the study was to be responsive to immediate needs, a different research strategy was needed.

We therefore approached our study with a less ambitious, but potentially more relevant, set of objectives. Our overriding goal was to develop an information base about current practices in the area of jail mental health services, from which a set of principles for program design could be distilled. By identifying and assessing the alternative arrangements local jails had developed to meet the service needs of mentally ill inmates, we felt that a series of guidelines and recommendations could be drawn up to assist those jails that were just beginning to develop local programs or that were in the process of expanding or enriching their inmate mental health services.

Ideally, a representative sample of jails would also have been useful for such a project, in order to insure a broad mix of facilities with varying numbers of inmates, resources, and community characteristics. However, as our basic goal was not to describe the current availability of mental health services in all U.S. jails, a more closely targeted study sample was appropriate and desirable. That is, in order to identify the various approaches and operational characteristics of jail mental health programs, a limited but reasonably broad cross-section of jails was sufficient. This reasoning was what prompted us to focus on the sample of jails that sent representatives to the 1979 NIC workshops, and to supplement this sample with other jails to increase the range of variation in services provided, administrative auspices under which services were provided, and court involvement.

Our subsequent contacts with local service providers at professional meetings, and a close monitoring of the literature in this field, have confirmed our judgment that our sample of 43 jails encompassed the major types of mental health programs now available and constituted a broad cross-section of small and moderate-sized facilities. By design, we excluded the "mega-jails" of the type that exist in New York City, Chicago, Los Angeles, or any of the other major metropolitan areas in the United States. These systems of facilities, with inmate populations in the range of 4,000 to 8,500, are both quantitatively and qualitatively distinct *vis-à-vis* the vast majority of U.S. jails. The problems of developing and operating inmate mental health services for these jails warrant separate study. Our research deliberately focused on a few large- and medium-sized jails with inmate populations of less than several hundred inmates. Such facilities, as noted earlier, detain the vast majority of inmates in U.S. jails.

Given these overall study goals, our data collection and analysis activities focused on five core questions:

1. *What kinds of services currently exist to meet the needs of mentally ill jail inmates?* To answer this question, we compiled detailed profiles of the range and mix of mental health services that were available for jail inmates in each of our study sites. Our interest here was in identifying the variety of practices in our sample that reflected the distinctive approaches to service delivery currently existing in this field.

2. *Does the way in which services are organized make a difference in the operation and perceived effectiveness of jail mental health programs?* To answer this question, we classified the mental health programs at each study site in terms of their administrative auspices (jail vs. mental health agency) and location (inside vs. outside the jail), and surveyed participants about the extent to which the programs were successful in meeting both safety and service goals.

3. *How did each of the programs fare during a 12- to 18-month follow-up period?* This question was addressed by conducting a telephone follow-up at each site to learn about any changes that occurred in the mental health services provided to jail inmates, developments in the community or state that impinged on the jail program (either positively or negatively), and budgetary cutbacks that led to the curtailment of inmate mental health services.

4. *What are the frequency and scope of disagreements between mental health and correctional personnel involved in the day-to-day operation of the jail mental health service program?* The issue of whether or not there is an enduring conflict between custody and therapy goals in correctional mental health services settings is one to which we became sensitized during the course of our research. Little research has addressed this issue for local jails. To answer this question, we resurveyed the respondents to our first questionnaire (the one on perceived effectiveness) with our second questionnaire (the one focused on potential day-to-day conflicts).

5. *Are there any principles for developing jail mental health services that are so fundamental as to be applicable to all jails?*

After examining the other four questions with data from the 43 jails, we hoped to be able to distill some basic guidelines that would be general enough to have broad application, but would also be practical enough to be usable by any community reviewing its mental health services for jail inmates.

The remainder of this book is devoted to a presentation of our findings with regard to each of these questions and related issues. In Chapter 2, as background for a consideration of our study findings, we review current standards for jail mental health services as promulgated by various professional associations. This review represents one of the most comprehensive assessments of professional standards currently available. It has value in its own right as a compilation and comparison of current standards, and can be read with benefit independently of the remainder of the book. Our basic contention is that although standards are important for insuring more effective responses to the problems of the mentally ill in jails, they fail to address many of the practical problems in a variety of jail settings. To develop such program design principles, research of the sort we have undertaken is needed.

Chapter 3 describes the mental health services that were available in our study sites at the time of our initial fieldwork. We present information about the frequency and mix of services provided by the 43 jails, and identify four distinctive approaches to service delivery that were followed by several of the study jails. To illustrate the substance of these approaches, we also present two capsule profiles of each type drawn from our site visits.

Chapter 4 addresses the perceived effectiveness of the various organizational arrangements for providing inmate mental health services in our study sites. We analyze the responses to our initial sample survey concerning the extent to which the administrative auspices and locations of jail mental health services made a difference in their perceived effectiveness and in the extent of interagency conflict associated with jail mental health programs. We also highlight the tradeoffs associated with the alternative organizational arrangements for delivering jail mental health services.

Chapter 5 focuses on the frequency and scope of conflict between mental health and correctional personnel in our study sites. Our findings are presented in the context of prior research on custody–therapy issues in prisons and mental hospitals, and the extent to which findings from this literature can be extrapolated to local jails. As will be seen, we found a consistency in goals between mental health and correctional staffs that does not support the previous findings of inherent staff conflict in studies of prisons.

Chapter 6 addresses subsequent developments and changes that impinged upon our study sites in the 12–18 months following our initial site visits. Findings are presented on changes in staff and service providers; program developments for the small, medium-sized and large jails; changes in specific services; and the role of litigation in jail mental health programs.

Chapter 7 presents our summary and conclusions concerning study findings and their implications for mental health program planning for local jails. Our recommendations are couched in terms of five basic principles focusing on the strategic choices that must be confronted by any local community in responding to the needs of mentally ill jail inmates. These principles represent a series of conceptual and practical guidelines for developing service programs that can be responsive to the serious human needs associated with the mentally ill in local jails. We have chosen to focus on core principles or guidelines for planning services, rather than isolating a few model programs that could be mirrored elsewhere. Consistent with Bachrach's (1980) observations of the disjuncture between actual, ongoing mental health systems and artificial model programs, we have become convinced that immense variations across the nearly 3,300 U.S. jails can be better addressed by adapting basic principles to local circumstances than simply by importing an entire model program. Ultimately, the specification of the five principles proposed in Chapter 7 should permit any given locality to develop and implement the type of program that best fits its needs and resources.

Chapters 8, 9, and 10 describe ongoing jail programs that exemplify how our basic planning principles can be reflected in practice. The first example is a jail suicide prevention program recently developed in the state of New York. The second is a description of a broader county-level community forensic program in which the jail is but one part. This Palm Beach County, Florida, program and the Boulder County, Colorado, program (described in Chapter 10) both highlight the importance of conceptualizing the mentally ill in local jails as a community-wide problem requiring community-wide solutions, not just a discrete program inside the jail.

The final chapter, Chapter 11, is a brief primer for mental health professionals who may provide services to jail inmates. Without (we hope) being condescending, we attempt to note some of the particular constraints placed on the delivery of mental health services and show how they can be dealt with effectively so as to not compromise the integrity of the mental health staff. Given the lack of experience of the mental health education system with local jails, this topic seems necessary and an appropriate note on which to conclude this book.

II

A NATIONAL STUDY

Chapter 2

Developing Services versus Generating Standards

Programmatic responses to the needs of mentally ill jail inmates have tended to be segmented and devised in particular localities for immediate problems. Neither empirical research nor professional associations have developed general models for jail mental health programs. Research has tended to focus on the narrow questions of the incidence of mental disorder in single jails (Petrich, 1976; Swank & Winer, 1976; Schuckit *et al.*, 1977). Professional associations, reflecting the interests of their members, have concentrated on program standards, usually emphasizing the need for their members to be the key providers. The result, as Brodsky (1982) has noted, is that "they [jail standards] do not specify the nature or patterns of such service delivery. . . . The standards do not offer guidelines but rather minimum criteria for program concerns and goals" (p. 144).

Jail administrators, county planning officers, or county mental health directors are left adrift when seeking guidance in developing jail mental health services. They have access to various standards, but guidelines for program development are exceedingly scarce. This is not to say that the standards are not useful; rather, it is to say that they are terribly limited in providing an adequate basis for developing the types of services needed for mental health care in local jails today. The standards may constitute a useful first step for planners, but they are little more than that—a first step.

Our intention in this chapter is to provide an overview of the major jail mental health standards that currently exist. The

21

presentation clearly shows why the field must begin to develop general principles for improving service delivery. The principles gleaned from our research may begin to fill this void and are detailed in Chapter 7. But before reviewing current standards for jail mental health services and assessing their actual usefulness, it may be useful first to define clearly what a jail is.

WHAT IS A JAIL?

The U.S. Department of Justice (1980b) defines a jail as "a locally administered confinement facility authorized to hold persons awaiting adjudication and/or those committed after adjudication to serve sentences of one year or less" (p. 1). This definition excludes drunk tanks and facilities designed specifically for the detention of juveniles. Also excluded are facilities operated by federal or state correctional authorities, including state-operated jails in Alaska, Connecticut, Delaware, Hawaii, Rhode Island, and Vermont. Police detention centers, where a person may be held for up to 48 hours following arrest, are likewise excluded, despite the fact that articles by Schleifer and Derbyshire (1968) and others inappropriately use the term "jail" to describe such lockups.

In many respects, the jail is the most important of all our institutions of imprisonment, since two-thirds to three-fourths of all convicted criminals serve their sentences in jails. The jail is also, with rare exceptions, the universal place of detention for untried prisoners and is used on occasion to retain key witnesses, children in need of supervision, mentally ill persons awaiting transfer to a state hospital, parole violators, and any number of other individuals who deviate from social norms.

Seventy-four percent of all American jails are run by counties; 22% are run by cities; and 4% are managed through a joint agreement between a city and a county. Responsibility for the operation of a county jail is usually assigned to the sheriff. More often than not, the sheriff has a stronger background in policing than in corrections and is primarily concerned with various aspects of law enforcement (patrolling rural areas, investigating crime, executing warrants, etc.). Day-to-day administration of jail management is typically delegated to deputies in all but the smallest jurisdictions.

Unlike long-term prisons, jails have never had a mandate to rehabilitate inmates or provide substantial programming opportunities. Such an endeavor would be impossible at most sites in any case, because of very limited funding and antiquated facilities. As noted earlier, nearly half of all jails are more than 30 years old ("New Jails," 1984), and 15% have not been renovated in over 15 years (American Correctional Association, 1978). The primary function of the jail is simply to detain persons awaiting trial and to incarcerate certain short-term criminals. Therefore, safety and security concerns are necessarily of paramount importance, and rehabilitation is almost never an issue.

THE GENESIS OF JAIL
MENTAL HEALTH STANDARDS

Had the states played a greater role in developing and enforcing meaningful guidelines in the first place, the development of standards by professional associations for jail mental health programs might not have been necessary. Forty-six states have jail standards of some type, but much of the content of these concerns generic safety and cleanliness requirements that are expected of all public institutions (Henderson, 1981). When such standards do address substantive inmate concerns, they tend to be so vague and minimal in nature that their benefit is often open to question. Every state that issues jail standards, for example, addresses the issue of medical services, while a few specify that professional staff and an on-site infirmary should be provided at facilities of a particular size. The most common provision, however, insists only that medical services be "regularly available" (Buckman, 1978).

Whether or not jailers comply with the most modest state expectations is often a moot point, because state efforts to monitor jail conditions are almost always lax. Twelve states have no jail inspection programs of any type (Ford & Kerle, 1981), and fewer than half of the states have established clear enforcement mechanisms (Henderson, 1981). Furthermore, many of the states that do inspect local jails only assign one or two people to this task (O'Neil, 1978).

The failure of the states to develop and enforce a significant body of jail standards can be attributed to a widespread legislative reality: A written set of abstract statements indicative of good intentions is far less volatile than a state agency empowered to interfere with local policy. Moreover, since responsibility for most jails in the United States falls under the jurisdiction of the politically powerful county sheriff, implementation could still be effectively thwarted in many locations even if state jail standards were more specific.

Officials interested in improving jail mental health services have thus frequently been unable to depend on the states for either guidance or supervision. And inasmuch as it has appeared highly unlikely that this situation will change markedly in the foreseeable future, several professional organizations have decided to promulgate operational standards of their own. The first to enter the field was the American Public Health Association (APHA), which did so in response to its overall mandate to improve the quality of general health care. The development of standards became a formal goal in 1972, and 4 years later the executive board approved the final draft submitted by a special task force on jails and prisons. *Standards for Health Services in Correctional Institutions* (APHA, 1976) contained only six principles specifically related to mental health programming, but the APHA's efforts represented an important first step and served as a basis for the formulation of more comprehensive standards in the years that followed.

The origin of the American Medical Association's (AMA's) involvement with jail standards can also be traced to 1972, when the organization conducted a national survey of local correctional facilities to identify areas of needed improvement in the delivery of inmate medical care. In June 1975, the AMA received a grant from the Law Enforcement Assistance Administration to address some of the more glaring deficiencies that the survey had documented. The project had three principal objectives: (1) to develop model health care delivery systems in jails at several pilot sites around the country; (2) to establish a clearinghouse for the dissemination of information and technical assistance; and (3) to prepare a series of jail health care standards that could be used for implementing a national accreditation program (Anno, Hornung, & Lang, 1981). In March 1979, the AMA published the first edition of *Standards for Health Services in Jails.* (The second edition [AMA, 1981] is the one referred to subsequently in this chapter.)

While still in the process of gathering information for use in drafting the standards, the AMA sought the assistance of the American Association of Correctional Psychologists (AACP). It was subsequently agreed that Robert Levinson, then president of the AACP and director of psychological services for the Federal Bureau of Prisons, would be given a seat on the AMA's special advisory committee. Levinson felt that the final version of the AMA standards had lost much of the impact and creativity of earlier drafts, and he encouraged the AACP to compile its own correctional standards. The final product, "Standards for Psychological Services in Adult Jails and Prisons," was released in March 1980.

During the AMA deliberations, the American Correctional Association (ACA) published the first edition of *Standards for Adult Local Detention Facilities* in 1977. (The second edition [ACA, 1981] is the one referred to subsequently in this chapter.) At that time the ACA was, and continues to be, the largest and most influential organization of corrections professionals in the country, so it came as no surprise when the ACA made guidelines available for the overall management of local jails. Like the standards proposed by the U.S. Department of Justice, those of the ACA address a number of administrative issues in addition to the narrower topic of inmate medical care.

In December 1980, the U.S. Department of Justice issued a series of guidelines under the title of *Federal Standards for Prisons and Jails.* These standards were reportedly written to help the department maintain consistency in federal correctional programs, and constituted one part of a bigger project to develop a comprehensive federal corrections strategy.

The most significant recent initiative in the area of jail mental health standards was the incorporation in 1982 of the National Commission on Correctional Health Care. This organization represented the formalization of the AMA's correctional health care program into a separate accrediting entity. This commission brought together 28 professional groups, ranging from the AMA to the American Bar Association, the American Psychiatric Association, and the National Sheriffs Association. Beyond its primary goal of accreditation, the commission also focused on education, training, and research.

Upon the inception of the commission's accreditation program in November 1983, 150 jails and 1 state prison were then certified under AMA standards. As of July 1987, a total of 268 correctional facilities were certified: 200 jails, 45 prisons, and 23 juvenile facilities. In 1987, the commission updated the AMA standards for health services for both jails and prisons. Through its accreditation program, published standards, and annual fall conference on health care, the National Commission on Correctional Health Care has become the primary resource for jail mental health standards information in the United States. There is simply no other regularly supported public or private agency that provides continuing resources in the area of correctional mental health standards.

The interest in correctional standards that emerged during the 1970s cannot be attributed solely to the concern about deinstitutionalization and its impact on jail mental health care. In fact, there was much more concern about general medical care than about mental health services in particular. The 1972 AMA survey had confirmed the worst fears of knowledgeable observers and shocked many authorities who had no idea how poor medical care in jail really was. The survey found that 17% of all jails had no internal medical facilities at all and that another two-thirds had only a first aid station. Just over half had a physician available on an on-call basis. At 31% of the jails, *no* physician was available to treat inmate needs (Steinwald, 1973).

Another major factor in the emergence of these various standards was the fact that the courts were beginning to intervene on behalf of inmates alleging cruel and unusual punishment.

Judges had traditionally been reluctant to interfere with internal correctional policies on the grounds that jail superintendents had far more expertise in such matters. They had, therefore, adopted a "hands-off" approach for all but the most intolerable cases. This policy began to change in the early 1960s, when Black Muslim prisoners persuaded the courts that their constitutional rights to religious freedom was being routinely violated. Successful litigation spread from suits based on the First Amendment's guarantee of religious freedom to suits based on other constitutional guarantees, and it soon became clear that the denial of adequate medical care was implicitly forbidden by the Eighth Amendment (Winner, 1981). Thus, while jail officials would probably have been very concerned about the welfare of mentally ill prisoners in any case, the task of developing standards to meet those concerns was given greater impetus by a number of unrelated factors.

In the remainder of this chapter, the actual standards of the different associations are examined, in order to determine their recommendations, their differences, and the extent to which they represent viable planning tools for jail administrators. The discussion focuses on the standards proposed by the AMA, the ACA, and the AACP.

Each standard has been assigned a level of importance by the sponsoring organization. The AMA and the AACP use an "essential–important" dichotomy. The ACA also describes certain standards as being either essential or important, but it also has a third "mandatory" category for those standards that must be implemented in order for a facility to receive ACA accreditation.

One of the principal conceptual problems that had to be addressed during the early development of all these standards concerned the level of care to be described. Some authorities argued that the standards should reflect minimally acceptable practices, so that administrators would know what they had to do to satisfy basic legal and ethical obligations. Others insisted that the standards should reflect optimal practices, to serve as a guide for those who wished to develop truly superior services. The latter approach was ultimately rejected as being an unrealistic vehicle for reform. Inasmuch as most officials lack the funding to implement an ideal set of procedures, it was felt that an ideal body of standards would have little to offer those who were seeking interim measures of improvement.

CORRECTIONAL MENTAL HEALTH CARE STANDARDS

Administration

First, it must be noted that many of the guidelines for mental health services really are generic statements for all health care in jails and are not specific to mental health services. A major goal of all the standards is to promote an administrative framework that establishes clear lines of authority and insures maximum cooperation between custodial and health care personnel. At a minimum, each job title filled at the jail should have a written job description so that there is no confusion regarding the exact role that each individual should play.

There is a unanimous belief that while medical and mental health professionals should adhere to all security regulations applicable to other facility staff members, they should also have clear authority to make and implement those decisions that they believe are in the best interests of the inmates. The APHA (1976) takes the position that this objective can best be accomplished when noncorrectional personnel are used to provide evaluation and treatment services:

> All health care service units in correctional institutions should ultimately be accountable to a governmental agency whose primary responsibility is health care delivery rather than the administration of such institutions. It is felt that health agencies are more likely to possess the competence to evaluate and conduct health programs than those agencies whose expertise is in security and custody. Accountability to such an agency aids in promoting and maintaining the integrity and excellence of health services. (p. viii)

None of the other standards takes an explicit position as to whether or not an external agency should be designated as the sole or primary provider of professional inmate care. The AACP does, however, recommend that the structure of the organization represent psychological services as a separate entity and that the unit budget be controlled by the chief psychologist.

The separation of professional and custodial responsibilities is a key concept that underlies many of the recommendations found in the standards. The AMA and the AACP, in particular, stress that health care personnel should not be called upon to provide services for the sole purpose of facilitating inmate management. Examples of the inappropriate use of professional resources include asking medical or mental health staff to provide special housing in the infirmary for homosexuals or informers, to conduct body-cavity searches for contraband substances, and to apply physical restraints to disruptive inmates who are not mentally ill. Talking to a "troublemaker" is likewise inappropriate when the inmate is simply angry rather than psychologically disturbed. According to the AACP, professional assistance should be offered only if staff action will directly benefit the inmate. Intervention that may be indirectly helpful to the prisoner is probably a management strategy and is less likely to be within the province of psychological services.

All of the standards maintain that the principle of confidentiality, which exists in noninstitutional settings, should likewise be applied in local detention facilities. They all indicate that health records should be maintained separately from the general confinement records and that all access to the records should be controlled by the chief treatment professional. Other recommendations as to how this principle should be applied vary greatly in their specificity. The issue of implementation is a crucial one, because many jail psychologists work for the sheriff, and an inmate's legal status can be seriously compromised if information obtained in a therapeutic relationship is eventually divulged to legal authorities.

The ACA and the AMA discuss confidentiality primarily in the context of health records. According to the ACA standard

(1981, p. 78), the health authority should share with the facility administrator information regarding "an inmate's medical management, security and ability to participate in programs." The AMA standard (1981, p. 42) does not specify any exceptions to the rule of confidentiality, but the ensuing discussion also refers to the desirability of sharing information relevant to "medical management and security." The APHA (1976, p. 30), in applying somewhat more rigorous criteria, asserts that the only exceptions to the rule of full confidentiality should be the "normal legal and moral obligations to respond to a clear and present danger of grave injury to self or others and the single issue of escape." Satisfactory compliance includes having the therapist explain the guarantee of confidentiality to his or her client, as well as the "precise delineation" of the foregoing limits. The therapist should also periodically review the guarantee and its limits to insure continued awareness. The official position of the AACP (1980, p. 98) is noncommittal: "A written policy exists and is implemented which outlines the degree to which confidentiality of information can be assured." Subsequent comments in the discussion, however, closely parallel the recommendations of the APHA. The ACA and AMA do not implicitly or explicitly indicate that inmates should be made aware of confidentiality limitations.

The decision to adopt a strict interpretation of confidentiality does not, of course, preclude a high degree of cooperation among correctional personnel, the facility administrator, medical staff, and related professionals. The AMA and the ACA recommend that the superintendent and chief health authority meet at least quarterly to discuss mutual concerns and the optimal use of resources. The AACP also endorses this practice, but suggests that the meetings be scheduled on a monthly basis. The ACA and the AACP further suggest that the health authority or chief psychologist submit a quarterly report to the facility administrator. The report should include comments on such issues as the effectiveness of the health care system, a description of any health-related environmental factors in need of improvement, changes effected since the last reporting period, and, if necessary, recommendations for corrective actions. The AACP and APHA also recommend that professional staff participate in the preparation and implementation of facility-wide planning. These organizations note that it is important for mental health personnel to view themselves and be viewed by others in the facility as part of the institution's total operation. However, mental health professionals who participate in administrative decision-making processes, such as approving inmates for work release, should not also be expected to provide direct therapeutic services.

The standards all make similar recommendations regarding day-to-day communication between correctional staff and medical and mental health staff. Specifically, written policy should require joint consultation before either group orders changes in the housing or programming assignments of inmates who have been diagnosed as having significant medical or psychiatric illnesses. They should also consult with each other whenever such inmates are being considered for transfers or are about to be punished for disciplinary infractions. A good working relationship will insure that medication does not endanger the safety of inmates who perform potentially hazardous maintenance tasks and that transportation staff receive proper instructions for transporting disturbed prisoners to other facilities.

Staffing and Professional Development

The standards unanimously recommend that someone be specifically designated as the chief medical and mental health authority. This person should be responsible for insuring that needed care is arranged in a timely manner and that adequate supplies are routinely available. He or she is also expected to make plans for future service development and to supervise the professional staff. The AMA (1981, p. 2) would like to see this role filled by a "physician, health administrator or agency," whereas the ACA (1981, p. 68) refers more generically to a "health authority." Both organizations suggest that this person oversee environmental conditions, the delivery of medical and dental services, personal hygiene, and dietary services, as well as overseeing mental health programming.

The AACP (1980, p. 89) stands alone in insisting that a psychologist be named to administer psychological services: "While it may be argued that good managers can be effective regardless of their degree of knowledge of the area being managed, this standard rejects such a contention. Efficient management is predicated on *both* expertise concerning psychological services and management skills" (emphasis in the original). Consequently, the AACP specifies that the person in charge of psychological services have a doctorate in a program that is "primarily psychological," in addition to having "appropriate training and experience." Although there is a difference of opinion as to the type of background that would be most useful in this position, the standards do agree that the responsibility should not be assigned to an officer or a correctional administrator.

The provision of timely care at many of the larger jails will require that the health authority or chief psychologist be assisted by other professional personnel. The standards provide mixed guidance, however, on staffing. The AMA (1981, p. 6) states only that there should be "adequate staff . . . as determined by the health authority," and gives this a rating of "important." According to the ACA (1981, p. 70), the facility should "systematically determine its personnel requirements in all categories on an on-going basis to ensure inmate access to staff and the availability of support services," and this is seen as "essential." Only the AACP offers what it considers an "essential" minimum ratio of inmates to staff. If the average daily population is less than 10, a psychologist should be on call. Jails with an average daily population of 11–75 should have a psychologist at the facility for at least 8 hours a week. If there are between 76 and 125 prisoners, the psychologist should be at the facility at least 16 hours a week, and when the population exceeds 125, the jail reportedly needs a minimum of one full-time psychologist. The AACP (1980, p. 95) has an additional expectation that the number of psychological services staff will increase "as the levels of special needs and/or program intensity differs from the average."

It is strongly suggested by all of the standards that state licensing and other certification requirements be applied to health care personnel at the jail and that verification of each person's credentials be kept on file. Professionals employed by federal, state, and local governments have been exempted in the past from statutes that establish minimal occupational qualifications, but this practice is clearly inconsistent with the stated goal of making the quality of inmate care as high as possible.

The use of inmates to provide health care services is virtually forbidden. All standards prohibit prisoners from giving direct patient care, scheduling health care appointments, determining the access of other inmates to health care, and handling medication. The AACP would also ban inmates from being involved in administering psychological tests, scoring the tests, and filing psychological data.

The need for technical training is recognized as "essential" and addressed at length by all the standards. It is recommended that professionals receive two types of instruction. The first consists of an orientation to the facility and an overview of how medical and mental health personnel function in a correctional setting. The AACP states that the orientation should be given to new employees during their first month of employment, while the ACA maintains that it should be completed before an individual is assigned to function independently in a particular job. Some form of continuing education is also needed so that the staff members can keep their skills up to date and stay informed of significant developments in their field. A training plan should be prepared that is consistent with the requirements of relevant state licensing boards. Such a plan should outline both the amount and frequency of the instruction needed for each staff position. The ACA is alone in specifying the number of hours that should be allotted for professional training: 40 hours of orientation, another 40 hours during the first year of service, and 40 hours each year thereafter.

Making arrangements for basic and in-service training of correction officers should also be a top priority for facility administrators. The standards suggest that officers be taught how to recognize the signs and symptoms of mental illness, what actions to take when responding to medical or psychological emergencies, how to refer inmates to the mental health unit for services, and what procedures to follow when transferring inmates to inpatient psychiatric facilities. In addition, the ACA and AMA recommend that officers be trained in the proper administration of medication. Although officer training obviously encompasses a number of topics unrelated to mental health, the ACA proposes that officers receive a total of 40 hours each year thereafter. According to the AACP, the chief psychologist should have the specific responsibility of seeing that all facility staff members have an understanding of basic mental health care.

The Identification and Management
of the Mentally Ill

All of the standards rank intake screening as one of the most significant mental health services that a jail can offer (it is ranked as "important" by the AMA and "essential" by the other two organizations). This assessment is usually described as a three-part process. First, the booking officer should review any papers or records that accompany the prisoner. The second step involves asking the inmate a series of questions about his or her mental health history. The questions should determine whether the individual has ever attempted suicide, been admitted to a psychiatric hospital, or committed acts of sexual deviancy. The officer should also try to ascertain whether there is a pattern of violence or of substance abuse and whether the inmate is currently taking any medication. Finally, the officer should record any visual observation of the inmate's behavior. Of particular interest are signs of delusions, hallucinations, peculiar speech and posturing, disorganization, depression, memory deficits, and evidence of self-mutilation. In addition to developing standards for the intake process, the AMA has prepared a model form for the specific purpose of screening incoming prisoners.

Although the implementation of a screening procedure is widely encouraged, it is designed only to identify disturbed inmates who respond to mental health questions accurately or who manifest overt signs of mental illness while being booked.

It is thus possible that inmates with serious psychiatric problems will still go undetected. It is also possible that the stress of the jail environment or uncertainty about an upcoming trial will cause some prisoners to break down after they have been admitted. One strategy to identify all inmates in need of services is the training of correction officers to recognize the symptoms of mental illness. Another, which the standards unanimously recommended, is that inmates be granted unhindered access to medical and mental health personnel. Inmates should receive written notice at the time of admission of the procedures to be followed for requesting psychological services. The AMA and ACA also recommended that a thorough health assessment be completed for each inmate within 14 days after arrival at the facility. The exam should be primarily medical in orientation, although the opportunity should be used to collect additional information for completing the psychiatric history.

Formal evaluations can be of an emergency or nonemergency nature. The AMA and AACP recommend that an assessment of an inmate referred for comprehensive psychological evaluations on a nonemergency basis be completed within 14 days. In an emergency, there is a consensus that the inmate should be held in a special area with constant supervision by trained personnel while waiting to receive professional attention. According to the AMA and the ACA, no more than 12 hours should elapse before emergency care is rendered. The AACP sets a deadline of 24 hours.

Once the evaluation has been completed, a decision must be made whether or not the inmate should be referred for appropriate care to some sort of mental health specialty unit. The AACP (1980, p. 103) calls for the referral of any inmate "having mental problems." The AMA and the ACA propose a somewhat more limited policy. The AMA (1981, p. 10) urges jails to refer prisoners "with acute psychiatric and other serious illnesses as defined by the health authority." The ACA (1981, p. 73) recommends that a referral be made if the individual's "adaptation to the correctional environment is significantly impaired."

If an inmate requires psychiatric treatment beyond what can be provided at the jail, the standards agree that he or she should be transferred to a facility where the needed services can be obtained. It is important that the facility administrator and a responsible physician consult prior to the actual transfer. The AMA notes in its discussion of this standard that written operating procedures for routine transfers should include an assessment of the individual's suitability for travel. The discussion also suggests that special care be taken to set aside any medication that will be needed en route and that special instructions be provided for the transportation staff when appropriate. In a separate standard, the AACP specifies that an inmate being transferred should be restrained (if physical restraint is necessary) with the least restrictive means possible and be accompanied by a trained staff member.

Mental health officials may, of course, decide to keep the less seriously disturbed inmates at the jail. If so, the standards take the unanimous position that professional staff should have "adequate" space, equipment, supplies, and materials as determined by the health authority (or, in the view of the AACP, the chief psychologist). In the discussion section following its standard on the special handling of patients with acute illnesses, the AMA (1981, p. 10) also sets three conditions that should be met if psychiatric treatment is to be provided at the jail:

1. A safe, sanitary, humane environment as required by sanitation, safety and health codes of the jurisdiction;
2. Adequate staffing/security to help inhibit suicide and assault (i.e., staff within sight and sound of all inmates); and
3. Trained personnel available to provide treatment and close observation.

The AMA is also the only organization that sets specific requirements for the operation of an infirmary or hospital.

The AACP (1980, p. 108) states that it is "essential" for written, individualized treatment plans to be prepared for inmates requiring close medical or psychological supervision. The plan should include directions to nonmedical staff regarding their role in the "care and supervision" of the inmate. The AMA (1981, p. 30) also recommends that treatment plans be prepared, but assigns the task a rating of "important" rather than "essential." The ACA incorporates the development of treatment plans into a separate body of prison standards, but does not make any reference to the topic in its standards for local detention facilities.

The AACP has apparently concluded that the use of medication falls outside its area of expertise, and thus remains silent on the issue. Medication is, however, discussed at length by the AMA (1981, p. 38) and the ACA (1981, p. 77). Both assign their highest rating of importance ("essential" for the AMA, "mandatory" for the ACA) to the idea that psychotropic medication should be used only "when clinically indicated as one facet of a program of therapy" (ACA, 1981, p. 77). They also agree that the prescribing physician should re-evaluate each prescription prior to renewal and that stop-order time periods be required for all medications. Only the AMA discourages the long-term use of minor tranquilizers and explicitly forbids the use of psychotropic medication for disciplinary purposes.

It is not clear what types of treatment should be available to medical or mental health professionals for the purpose of selecting the other facets of therapy that will accompany medication. The basic philosophy underlying all of these standards is that the health care provided in institutions should be equivalent to that available in the community. The AMA and ACA, however, tend to be quite vague regarding the specific mental health treatment services that should be made available, and the AACP does not give its list of proposed services the strength of an actual standard. The APHA (1976, p. 31) recommends "varied modalities" and "eclectic breadth." At a minimum, satisfactory compliance with the APHA's standard on direct treatment requires that the facility provide crisis intervention, brief and extended evaluation/assessment, group and individual short-term therapy, group and individual long-term therapy, therapy with family and significant others, counseling, medication, inpatient hospitalization for the severely disturbed, and detoxification.

The standards concur that whatever the type of treatment to be used, the principle of informed consent as applied in a particular jurisdiction should likewise be applied for inmate care. The AMA and the ACA indicate that care can be rendered against an inmate's will only in accordance with state law, but the AACP would also require that the decision to apply coercive treatment be preceded by interdisciplinary review if time permits. The use of physical restraints should be controlled by all standards through the implementation of written policies that identify the authorization needed and specify when, where, for how long, and in what manner restraints may be applied. Formulation of the substantive content of these policies, however, is consistently left to the discretion of facility officials. Only the ACA categorically prohibits inmates' participation in medical and pharmacological experimentation, although the AACP notes that psychologists should "refuse to participate in practices inconsistent with legal, moral, and ethical standards regarding the treatment of clients" (1980, p. 102).

Finally, the AMA and the AACP stress the importance of continuing care from the time of admission to the date of discharge. As part of this general orientation, both organizations encourage arrangements for postrelease follow-up care in the community whenever circumstances warrant it.

THE USE OF STANDARDS TO DEVELOP JAIL MENTAL HEALTH SERVICES

Given the vast array of standards, where does this leave the planner of jail mental health services? Basically, he or she is left with a whole set of prescriptions, without any guidelines as to how to fit them together in a coherent program, how to initiate the program, and how to finance the program.

Organizational standards for jail mental health services were developed at a time when there was a great deal of confusion among jail administrators regarding how they should care for mentally ill inmates in their custody. Basic issues had not yet been clearly formulated, much less resolved, and it was not even clear which services would be judicially mandated. Officials were forced to improvise as best they could. One indicator of the contribution that organizations such as the AMA and the ACA have made is the fact that federal and state courts have since come to rely on their standards as a measure of culpability in suits alleging inadequate psychiatric treatment. In seeking to define the minimal level of care acceptable to medical and mental health professionals, the standards' authors have, in effect, established the touchstone against which jail services will be compared in court. Several judges have already ordered that local correctional facilities be brought into compliance with organizational standards in order to correct program deficiencies (Connors, 1979; Wilson, 1980).

Perhaps the single most important theme that emerges in the standards is the need for all health care services to be delivered in the context of a formal, structured program. Planning for mental health care, in particular, was traditionally very haphazard. More often than not, responsibility for mental health care was an implied responsibility of the jail's medical staff, and services were only arranged on an as-needed basis. The standards stress that this approach is no longer viable. Individual administrators may apply a certain recommendation in a variety of ways to conform with local tradition and circumstances, but all sources of assistance must be identified in advance of need so that care can be provided on a 24-hour basis. Once in place, moreover, policies and procedures must be reexamined at least annually and updated as appropriate. The AACP (1980, p. 93), in addition, calls for a "formal documented annual review" to be conducted by an outside agent to monitor conformity with the standards.

Although the standards are helpful tools, they have a number of limitations as well. To begin with, the standards do not always agree on the ways in which broad principles of care can best be implemented, as the preceding section has indicated. Another problem is that many of the standards are worded so broadly that very little actual guidance is provided. Although some generalization is necessary in order to make the standard as widely applicable as possible, the specific meaning of critical terms often remains unclear. For example, what constitutes an "adequate" amount of space and equipment for medical and mental health staff? What kinds of "training" and "accountability" are appropriate for volunteers? Who should be allowed to authorize the use of involuntary restraints? The standards uniformly call for standard operating procedures to guide mental health professionals in virtually all their activities, but the actual substance of these procedures is not always given sufficient attention.

Although some standards are, in fact, quite specific, they can often be overly demanding as well. It is significant to note in this context that the organizations that have drafted standards for services in jails also include some of the same recommendations in their standards for prisons. However, several experts have questioned the wisdom of this decision. Of the 3,300 jails in the United States, approximately half have a designated capacity of fewer than 10 inmates, while another 25% have between 10 and 20 beds (Miller, 1978). Furthermore, research conducted by Flint (1978) indicates that many of the planners who set jail standards seldom take the time to visit a rural facility. It is thus possible that planners do not fully appreciate the challenges involved in operating a small county jail. A glaring example is the "essential" ACA standard that correctional officers receive at least 40 hours of training annually. According to a 1982 national survey conducted by the National Sheriffs Association, 11% of all jails in the country do not have enough officers to provide 24-hour coverage (Kerle & Ford, 1982). And many of those that do have enough officers consider themselves fortunate if they can arrange to excuse personnel from duty long enough to attend a single in-service lecture during the course of a year.

The standards' authors have responded to charges of unrealistic expectations by saying that even if a given provision seems burdensome, it is still a necessary element in the delivery of minimal health care services. Whether a facility is small or large, rich or poor, certain core services must be made available. The fact remains, however, that most jails are old, understaffed, and underfinanced. And while there are undoubtedly valid medical reasons for requiring that psychotropic medication be administered only as one facet of a program of therapy, many administrators simply cannot afford to provide additional treatment. The net result is that many jails will never be able to qualify for AMA accreditation; only 192 jails (6%) were accredited as of September 1988.

Significant reform is elusive because of the chronic shortage of public funds and the indifference of many citizens to the plight of those who break the law. Complicating the situation still further is the fact that jails tend to operate in a highly politicized atmosphere. Hiring criteria and planning priorities are likely to be heavily influenced by any number of considerations that are only marginally related to the professional operation of the facility. At least part of the problem, however, can be attributed to what is perhaps the single biggest limitation of jail standards: They focus on content to the virtual exclusion of the form that is needed to implement that content. Administrators are told what to do, but not how to do it. Standards simply do not constitute a blueprint for the development of better services. Rather, they are statements of desirable goals that jail officials should try to meet as best they can.

In fairness, it should be noted that it is not really the intent of the standards to provide detailed instructions for implementation. Their sole purpose is to identify those policies and practices that should be followed when planning the delivery of jail mental health services. To help administrators implement the policies, the AMA standards indicate that a series of books is available, but these publications tend to lack the kind of specific detail that would be needed by officials to introduce new services with no outside help. Technical assistance is available for those who are able to pay for it, but, once again, jail authorities usually have very limited discretionary funds.

The major contribution of all jail mental health standards lies in the fact that they give planners of jail mental health programs a clear statement of objectives to guide their programming efforts. Many officials will still be left wondering, however, what they can or should be doing to obtain the recommended services. The AMA (1981, p. iii) recognizes that "reliance on community resources for manpower and facilities is the only way that most facilities can provide special services such as detoxification and psychiatric care." Nevertheless, very little attention has been paid thus far to the crucial variable of liaisons between correctional and mental health agencies. The next chapter suggests the usefulness of an interorganizational approach to specifying the structure of jail mental health programs, and lays the groundwork for a subsequent analysis of how these can be planned and implemented.

Chapter 3

Varieties of Jail Mental Health Programs

One of the goals of our research was to compile descriptive profiles of the range and mix of mental health services that were available for jail inmates at each of our study sites. This chapter provides an overview of our findings, with special attention to the distinctive service delivery approaches encountered at the time of our initial fieldwork. The information presented here serves as a detailed overview of our sample sites and background for the assessments of program effectiveness, program development, and staff conflict, all of which are considered in subsequent chapters.

In our depictions of these various approaches to jail mental health services, we have deliberately avoided use of the term "model programs." As noted in Chapter 1, models often tend to be somewhat idealized types that are difficult to fit into less-than-perfect, real-world systems of care (Bachrach, 1980). Furthermore, a major finding that emerged from our work, which is described in detail in Chapter 4, is that there is no one best way to arrange jail mental health services. The term "model programs," on the other hand, seems to imply that there *is* one best way, or perhaps a few best ways. Accordingly, in this chapter we discuss the four major approaches toward structuring jail mental health services that were observed across the 43 jails studied, and we highlight the content of these programs. Chapter 4 focuses more on the organizational arrangements for these services; it provides a close examination of how jails relate to the range of mental health agencies that do, or can, provide services to jail inmates.

CRITERIA FOR JAIL MENTAL HEALTH SERVICES

One of the initial problems we encountered in our study was the absence of clear definitions and criteria for "jail mental health services." Although most observers would argue that some type of mental health screening or case identification is a minimal service in a jail setting (e.g., Newman & Price, 1977a), we could find little consensus in the available literature about the range of other services that should be included. Accordingly, before conducting our initial site visits, we developed a broad definition of "jail mental health services" on the basis of available reports and the standards promulgated by professional associations as presented in Chapter 2. Nine possible services were included in this definition: (1) intake screening at booking, (2) evaluation following initial screening, (3) assessment of competency to stand trial, (4) use of psychotropic medications, (5) substance abuse counseling, (6) psychological therapy, (7) inpatient care, (8) external hospitalization, and (9) case management or linkage of inmates with community mental health agencies following release. Although competency evaluations are court-related assessments, we included them as a mental health service because psychiatric services for jail inmates are sometimes arranged, both overtly and covertly, as part of the competency examination process (Geller & Lister, 1978). All educational, legal, religious, social service, or other inmate activity programs not explicitly directed at the assessment or treatment of identifiable mental disorders or substance abuse problems were excluded from consideration.

   1. Intake screening is "a system of structured inquiry and observation designed to prevent newly arrived inmates who pose a health or safety threat to themselves or others from being admitted to the facility's general population and to get them

rapidly admitted to medical care" (AMA, 1981, p. 23). A study jail was considered to have a screening process if (a) new inmates were routinely asked questions pertaining to their mental health (past suicide attempts, prior psychiatric hospitalizations, etc.); (b) the questions were printed on a standard form, so that the booking officer would not have to rely on his or her memory to remember specific questions or would not forget to make the designated inquiries altogether; and (c) the screening form was completed during intake.

2. Psychological evaluations are assessments in which inmates receive a clinical interview with specific questions focusing on a particular characteristic or set of circumstances that may be affecting their behavior. A study jail was considered to have an evaluation service if mental health professionals assessed inmates suspected of being mentally ill on an as-needed basis for reasons unrelated to competency, presentencing investigations, or other court-related functions. The jail had to initiate the evaluation as part of its own service program; the need for evaluation was usually identified through intake screening.

3. Competency evaluations are court-mandated assessments to determine whether a defendant understands the circumstances surrounding his or her legal predicament and is able to cooperate with an attorney in his or her own defense. Jail officials cannot initiate such an evaluation, but the process occasionally occurs as the most effective way to get an inmate out of the jail and into a mental health facility. Study jails that held pretrial inmates who were given competency exams, either at the jails themselves or in mental health settings (e.g., a court clinic or state hospital), were recorded as having this service.

4. Psychotropic medications include the antipsychotics or major tranquilizers, such as Thorazine or Mellaril; antianxiety medications, such as Valium, that induce sedation; antidepressants, which encompass both barbiturates and amphetamines; and mood-stabilizing drugs, such as lithium, that are used for patients experiencing acute manic states. Study jails that used prescribed medications to stabilize disturbed inmates were considered to be offering this service, regardless of whether the medicine was distributed by correction officers or professional staff.

5. In order for a study jail to be viewed as providing substance abuse counseling for inmates, the therapy had to have a clear psychological orientation and be offered for the purpose of helping the client overcome a drug or alcohol problem. The counseling also had to be available to all inmates in need of it or to an appropriate subgroup, as determined by jail or mental health officials. If the counseling was not done at the jail, correctional officials had to provide the necessary transportation. It thus did not suffice to give inmates on work-release programs the option of obtaining outside counseling on their own. No minimum qualifications were established for the counselors in order for the site to be coded as having this service.

6. Psychological therapy in a study jail was defined as consisting of a clinical interaction between an inmate and a mental health professional having at least a master's degree, which was oriented toward the goal of helping the client make some improvement in his or her behavior. Although no restrictions were placed on form (individual vs. group) or style (Freudian vs. Rogerian), the therapy had to be scheduled in a way that permitted more than just a superficial exchange of comments. It would not suffice for a psychologist to seek out a particular inmate on an irregular basis to "see how things are going." Therapy would typically, although not necessarily, be given in the context of crisis intervention.

7. Inpatient care is a service provided for inmates whose illnesses are so acute that they can no longer be safely managed in a traditional correctional setting. The service is provided within the jail in an infirmary used in whole or in part to treat the mentally ill. A study jail was considered to be providing this service internally if infirmary beds were routinely used or reserved for disturbed inmates. The AMA's (1981) criteria for an infirmary had to be met in order for a jail to be given credit for offering internal inpatient care:

> An infirmary is an area established within the correctional facility in which organized bed care facilities and services are maintained and operated to accommodate two or more inmates for a period of 24 hours or more and which is operated for the expressed or

implied purpose of providing skilled nursing care for persons who are not in need of hospitalization. (p. 28)

8. External hospitalization may occasionally have to be arranged for inmates with serious long-term psychiatric needs or acute short-term needs that cannot be met within the jail. A jail was given credit for providing this service if seriously disturbed inmates were transferred to a local hospital, a state hospital forensic unit, or (in the case of nonviolent and low-risk inmates) to a civil unit within a state hospital.

9. Case management is a process in which inmates in need of mental health care at the time of release are linked with appropriate community agencies capable of providing ongoing treatment. A study jail was seen as providing a case management service if (a) appointments were made with mental health agencies for all mentally ill inmates or a specific subgroup (such as those receiving psychotropic medication), and (b) referrals were made for inmates with a variety of mental health problems. It did not suffice to give inmates the names and addresses of possible service providers or to make appointments just for those with substance abuse problems.

These nine services constitute the core elements of mental health programming in local jails. Some jails, however, may offer additional types of care or manage disturbed inmates in ways that are not readily included within the range of services just listed. Larger facilities, for example, may have the capability to segregate all new inmates for a period of 48–72 hours, so that correction officers will be better able to identify mentally ill offenders before they are placed in the general population. Other jails may have padded cells or special observation units for inmates whose behavior seems particularly erratic.

DISTRIBUTION OF SERVICES

As shown in Table 3.1, there was considerable variation in the number of jails in our study that provided each type of service. Every jail offered some type of psychotropic medication pro-

TABLE 3.1. Services Provided by Jail Mental Health Programs ($n = 43$)

Type of service	Number of jails providing service	Percentage of jails providing service
Mental health screening	30	70%
Evaluation	42	98%
Internal	13	30%
External	29	68%
Psychotropic medication	43	100%
Competency examinations	40	93%
Drug–alcohol treatment	26	60%
Therapy–counseling	13	30%
Inpatient care		
Internal and external	9	21%
External only	34	79%
Case management at release		
Substance abuse	16	37%
General mental health	7	16%

gram, and all had some procedures to transfer inmates to external inpatient hospital settings. In fact, the waiting lists at many state hospitals were so long that for many jails inpatient hospitalization was an option on paper only. Moreover, all but one jail were found to have some arrangement for obtaining a specialized mental health evaluation of inmates after the initial screening had indicated potential mental health problems. In 40 of the 43 jails, competency examinations were available. The remaining 3 jails only held inmates who had been convicted, so the issue of competency was not relevant.

Less frequently encountered program components were mental health screening at the time of admission (70%) and substance abuse counseling (60%). The services least often available were any type of therapy beyond medications (30%) and case management at time of release (16%), although it should be noted that what was termed "case management" by staff was as limited, in most cases, as giving the inmate the address and telephone number of the local community mental health center.

In general, jails tended to equate identification and treatment with the use of psychotropic medications. This is consistent with an orientation toward crisis stabilization, which is typical of facilities (such as jails) dedicated to the rapid turnover of persons with acute problems. Long-term treatment and referral of inmates to community services at release were infrequent. As one jail administrator observed in regard to case management, "Correctional officers don't care about what happens out on the street. Once the guy leaves, he's not their problem. He becomes a problem for the law enforcement agencies." At the same jail, another administrator noted, "If case management works well, [the correctional officers] don't see the results. Therefore, they don't appreciate the impact of those mental health services." Overall, then, the jails studied emphasized services that focused on the behavioral management of the inmate within the jail, and not on long-term mental health treatment concerns that might benefit the inmate while incarcerated or upon return to the community.

Although it was relatively easy to determine how many jails offered each type of mental health service, it was much more difficult to summarize the various ways in which jails made use of these individual services. Following our site visits, we carefully analyzed all field notes and interviews in order to categorize the approaches toward mental health services of the 43 jails we visited. The taxonomy that emerged from our review appeared to be a useful way of organizing the major types of programs we had seen. These categories and some examples of each are presented in the next section to provide a basis for understanding the analytic work on the interorganizational structure of these programs, as presented in Chapter 4, and for evaluating the principles for program development discussed in Chapter 7.

MAJOR APPROACHES TO JAIL MENTAL HEALTH PROGRAMS

From our site visits, we concluded that there existed four basic types of service arrangements for mentally ill inmates: (1) "ad hoc," in which virtually no services were offered except on an emergency basis; (2) "identification," in which correctional officials sought only to identify inmates who were disturbed; (3) "identification and treatment," in which inmates found to be mentally ill were also treated; and (4) "comprehensive," in which identification, treatment, and referral services were all available. Although other combinations of program options can be derived conceptually, these service types appeared to summarize succinctly the very wide range of programs that were studied.

Each approach had distinct goals, program characteristics, and underlying philosophy as to what a jail can and should do for the mentally ill. However, it should be kept in mind that the objectives associated with each type were not always as clearly defined in the minds of those responsible as our discussion of their underpinnings might seem to suggest. Policy makers at the sites sometimes followed a formal planning process in which a special task force did consider the various ramifications of modifying the existing service structure, but the mental health programs usually evolved somewhat haphazardly. For example, one jail hired a nurse who took the initiative to implement a new screening program, without any specific direction or encouragement from the sheriff to do so. The head nurse at another jail happened to meet a former schoolmate who had started working at the local mental health center, and the two agreed over lunch to join forces in developing a substance abuse program for sentenced inmates. Annual changes in the level of funding caused sudden or unexpected changes in the services at several sites. Thus, while jail administrators might never have formally decided just to identify the mentally ill as opposed to also treating them, the ongoing programs nevertheless did seem to sort themselves into the four distinct groups.

The Ad Hoc Approach

Jail officials who provided ad hoc psychological services made arrangements for mental health care on a case-by-case, as-needed basis. There was no systematic attempt to identify mentally ill prisoners, and little if any treatment other than medication was routinely made available while the inmates were incarcerated. Special care was offered only in emergency situations, such as a suicide attempt or psychotic episode. Disturbed prisoners about to be released were seldom if ever referred to agencies that could provide approriate care in the community.

The mental health goals of an ad hoc jail tended to be very modest: to stabilize severely disturbed prisoners, and to transfer to an inpatient psychiatric facility those inmates who could no longer be safely managed at the jail. Although correctional staff members did make a bona fide effort to react promptly in crisis situations, they did not see their role as one of anticipating less critical inmate needs and of intervening as soon as a potentially serious problem was detected. They acknowledged no responsibility for the mentally ill other than to insure the basic safety of the individual while in custody. The jail strove to meet its strict legal obligations but did not exceed them.

When someone was admitted to this type of jail, no effort was made to determine whether he or she would be able to make a satisfactory adjustment to the correctional environment. Routine intake procedures varied only when an inmate was totally disoriented to time and place, or had been held at the jail before and was recognized as having a history of mental illness. Even then, clinical services were seldom arranged unless the inmate posed a serious threat to self and/or others. A common response was to make a note in the jail log indicating that the person should be watched a bit more closely than usual.

If an inmate in the jail population began to exhibit signs of abnormal behavior, the initial staff reaction typically consisted of a "wait-and-see" posture. Any number of management techniques might be employed to keep potential disruptions to a minimum, but only when the behavior could no longer be ignored would professional assistance be sought. Medical personnel (often a licensed practical nurse or a paramedic) were usually asked to examine the prisoner to determine whether a formal evaluation should be scheduled, and, if so, whether it should be done on an emergency or nonemergency basis. If it was ultimately decided that inpatient care was required, the inmate would be transferred to an appropriate facility. Otherwise, the individual would be stabilized and given the minimum ongoing treatment necessary for maintenance.

Jails with an ad hoc mental health program offered very few services of any kind. High school equivalency diploma instruction and job counseling might be available to those who were interested, but such activities were the exception rather than the rule. Alcoholics Anonymous (AA) might also be allowed to conduct weekly meetings if there was a suitable room that could be reserved for this purpose. Substance abuse counseling was technically a form of treatment, but it was seldom used to help individual inmates overcome destructive drinking habits. Any prisoner who wished to attend an AA meeting was generally given permission, with no preliminary screening or prior determination of need.

Rural Southern Jail

A good example of a jail that provided mental health services on an ad hoc basis was located in a Southern state, in a county of approximately 30,000 residents. The facility had a rated capacity of 17 beds, but frequently held 25–30 prisoners because severe overcrowding in the state correctional system caused lengthy delays in the transfer of sentenced felons to prisons. The jail was operated by a sheriff who had been in office for 9 years.

The sheriff's jail staff consisted of four deputies and two transport officers, none of whom had any formal training. The sheriff did not have sufficient personnel to provide 24-hour coverage at the jail, so officers assigned to the county's road patrol checked the inmates periodically during the evening and early morning hours.

The political atmosphere in the surrounding community was very conservative. There was a widespread consensus that since inmates had willfully committed crimes, they should not expect to receive any nonemergency services while incarcerated. As a result, no activities were scheduled at the jail, except that a minister visited once a week for 30 minutes. The county had constructed a new jail in 1969 to provide better security and office space for the sheriff, but the cells in which the inmates were actually housed were taken from the old jail, which was built in 1902.

The sheriff saw no need to contract with a physician for services, preferring instead to rely on one of the jail deputies, who was an emergency medical technician. This deputy had the responsibility of arranging care for inmates who "flipped out." If a prisoner was in need of an immediate psychological evaluation, he or she would be brought to the emergency room of the county's only hospital. Nonemergency evaluations were scheduled at a satellite unit of a regional mental health center. Jail officials estimated that fewer than 1% of all inmates ever required an evaluation. According to the psychologist at the clinic, however, the jail would wait until the last possible minute to make an appointment, and only those in an acute state of crisis were ever brought to his attention. Even then, he generally concluded, the individuals were in a much worse condition than the jailers seemed willing to believe. Interestingly, the inmates were eventually billed for the cost of this evaluation. Since most did not pay, the county was considering a proposal to impose a $1.00 charge in advance so that at least some of the "malingerers" could be eliminated.

Inmates who required inpatient psychiatric treatment were sent to one of two state hospitals. Use of the first facility was limited because it did not have a locked ward. Admitting doctors were reluctant to accept inmates who might pose a threat to others, and the jail was reluctant to send inmates there because of the lack of security. It was not against the law in this state for a prisoner to escape from a mental institution, so escapes were frequent. The second hospital available to the jail did have a secure unit. Several other local correctional facilities were also located within the hospital's catchment area, however, and since bed space was very limited, there was often an 8-month waiting period to get someone admitted. Jail officials conceded that they did not provide adequate care for psychotic inmates awaiting transfer. According to the sheriff, the only reason that the jail had not been placed under a court order was that "no one has bothered to file suit."

Urban Midwestern Jail

The second example of ad hoc jail services was located in a Midwestern state, in a county with 150,000 inhabitants. This facility had an average daily population of 128, which was just within the designated capacity. Operation of the facility was officially the responsibility of the county sheriff.

In 1978, this jail had entered into a far-reaching consent decree that had an impact on a variety of areas, including the quality of food, availability of law books, opportunities to exercise, and visiting regulations. Under the terms of the agreement, the jail was also expected to provide nonemergency psychiatric care within 48 hours to inmates who requested it. Despite the apparent need for major changes in jail operations, the county board of supervisors had recently rejected the sheriff's requests for additional funds. Included in that request was a proposal to hire an outside consultant to assess inmates' mental health needs. At the time of the site visit, jail officials were preparing to go to court to answer charges that they had violated the decree.

The jail employed 25 sworn deputies, 7 nonsworn correction officers, and 8 support staffers. None of the custodial staff had received any formal training. The jail also employed a nurse 1 day a week. The policy manual indicated that the nurse was expected to examine all newly admitted inmates within 1 week, but other, more pressing responsibilities often precluded this practice.

The jail administrator did not believe that the facility needed an extensive mental health program. Recent changes in state law allowed police officers who arrested someone suspected of being mentally ill to take that individual directly to a mental health facility. This procedure was reportedly successful in preventing the "obvious crazies" from being brought to the jail. The administrator felt that fewer than 1% of all inmates ever needed a psychological evaluation in any case. In those rare instances when the need did arise, the shift supervisor could make an appointment at the county mental health center. A private psychiatrist was on call for the four or five emergencies that might occur in the jail during the course of a year. Inmates had to be given a competency exam prior to trial were taken on the "mental run" to a state hospital.

If an inmate required inpatient psychiatric care, the jail claimed to have no difficulty in getting an admission to an appropriate facility. The local mental health center had an inpatient unit that was used to stabilize nonviolent inmates, and the more aggressive prisoners could be placed in a state hospital forensic unit. Jail officials doubted the inmates would be willing to participate in therapy sessions at the jail even if such counseling were available, because the prisoners were afraid of being labeled "nuts" by their peers.

The only nonessential service that the inmates received was provided by AA. Jailers insisted that most inmates attended AA only to get out of their cells, but allowed the program to continue, in deference to the wishes of an employee of the mental health center who did substance abuse evaluations of pretrial inmates for area courts. The chief administrator of the jail pointed with pride to the fact that the facility had not had a successful suicide attempt in 25 years as proof that his approach to mental health care was working.

The Identification Approach

The principal characteristic of jails with an identification approach was the attempt by correctional authorities to determine which inmates were mentally ill. Little treatment (other than medication and emergency-level care) was provided, but extra attention was frequently given to any prisoner who appeared to be disturbed and who might need such care in the future.

Mental health programming at jails oriented toward the identification of the mentally ill emphasized the following: (1) identifying inmates with serious psychological problems; (2) monitoring the condition of inmates whose behavior suggested that they were somewhat unstable; (3) stabilizing acutely disturbed prisoners; and (4) transferring inmates to a psychiatric facility whenever inpatient care was required. The goals were actually quite similar to those found in the ad hoc jails. Authorities in both were interested in protecting the lives of the mentally ill and those of the people with whom the mentally ill came in contact, but the strategies used to accomplish these goals in both approaches did not include treatment in nonemergency situations. The identification model was distinguished primarily by the efforts of jail staff to determine in advance of crisis situations whether inmates were mentally ill. Information gathered during the identification process was intended to help officials manage the jail better, rather than to serve as a basis for correcting any psychological imbalance that was found.

Identification services typically included some form of screening at intake. By gathering information on an inmate's mental stability before he or she was assigned to the general population, jail staff members hoped that they would be better able to decide whether the mentally ill individual should be placed in isolation from the outset or assigned to a regular cell with more supervision than usual. Officials at the ad hoc jails expected their staff to make similar judgments without such procedures or special training.

Urban Southeastern Jail

One jail with a mental health program geared toward the identification of disturbed inmates was situated in the third largest county (300,000 people) of a Southeastern state. This facility officially had the capacity to house 129 inmates, but the daily population was usually closer to 140. Administration of the jail fell under the jurisdiction of a county sheriff. The sheriff, in turn, had appointed an individual with a master's degree in public administration to serve as the jail's chief of operations. The only other noncustodial staff members were two licensed practical nurses.

When the jail was built in 1971, facility planners expected that it would only be used to incarcerate prisoners who would be in custody for a few weeks. There were few delays then in scheduling court appearances, and the state department of corrections promptly assumed custody of inmates receiving sentences of more than 30 days. It did not appear to be either necessary or logical to allot space for inmate programming of any type. But initial perceptions were not valid over the long run. In the years that followed, more and more offenders were incarcerated, and judges were no longer able to schedule hearings as quickly as they did when the jail was first designed. The average length of stay was nearly 4 months at the time of our site visit. Jail officials literally did not have any space to set aside specifically for the delivery of mental health services, despite the current need.

New prisoners were screened by booking officers for signs of mental illness and were then sent to the nursing station for a physical examination. All officers were required to take a 40-hour training program that included instruction in the nature of behavioral disorders and in the recognition of psychological disturbance. The nurses and chief of operations also attended periodic mental health training seminars whenever possible. Members of the line staff were not sent to these workshops because of the need to maintain adequate coverage at the jail, but they were kept informed of key points made during the various lectures, via informal conversations at lunch or in the cell block. The early identification of disturbed inmates was given a particularly high priority at this jail because of its location just 3 miles from a major state hospital. It was estimated that 30% of all prisoners brought to the jail had been previously admitted to the hospital and that 60% had mental-health-related problems.

Inasmuch as 95% of the inmates were awaiting trial, nearly all evaluations were handled as part of the process of determining competency to stand trial. When an inmate began to behave in an aberrant manner, the jail notified the inmate's attorney in the hope that he or she would obtain a court order to have the prisoner examined. In 1980, a total of 64 inmates were evaluated in this manner. A private psychiatrist could be asked to come to the jail to evaluate sentenced prisoners, but this option was seldom exercised except in emergencies.

Just prior to the site visit, the chief of jail operations had sought approval to hire a general resource person to oversee the delivery of mental health services and to hire a social worker to act as a liaison officer with county mental health agencies. Jail officials were successful in hospitalizing about 75% of all those whom they wished to have admitted, but the remaining 25% received virtually no care at all. The sheriff nevertheless refused to submit either proposal to the county legislature, because the county was facing a $15,000,000 reduction in federal funding. The county manager conceded that the quality of psychological care at the jail was "poor," but pointed out that the jail was still basically a short-term facility and that those truly interested in receiving treatment could obtain it at the mental health center when they were released. The director of the mental health center, meanwhile, viewed forensic services at the jail as a "Johnny-come-lately" and rejected the suggestion that the jail should be part of the center's responsibilities. He noted that delivery of service at the jail would be difficult in any case because the facilities were so noisy and cramped. What the jail needed most, in his opinion, was a mechanism for alleviating acute psychological distress and for making referrals at release so that clients could better take advantage of the area's mental health resources.

Urban Midwestern Jail

Another example of a jail where officials had implemented an identification process was located in the Midwest. The urban county that operated the jail had 309,000 residents. The sheriff had appointed a former chief of police with 30 years of law enforcement experience to run the jail on a daily basis.

The jail was built in 1973 to house 168 inmates. By 1981, the average daily population had reached 215, all but 15 of whom were awaiting trial. The county had responded to the over-crowding situation by forming a special task force to monitor conditions at the jail and to develop strategies for keeping the population within manageable levels. The task force's principal accomplishment at the time of our site visit had been to win approval for the construction of a new 80-bed work-release center. Although the county sent more people to prison on a per capita basis than any county in the state, the public was "very unwilling" to spend money for jail services. Since there were no state standards regulating the management of local correctional institutions, there was seemingly little reason to fund jail services beyond the minimal level needed for the safe operation of the facility.

It might be noted that this jail was similar in many ways to the previously described urban Southeastern jail. Both were overcrowded medium-sized facilities, held mostly pre-trial inmates, and had very limited public support to develop inmate services. Unlike the chief of operations at the first site, however, the jail director in this county was adamantly opposed to the presence of any full-time mental health staff at the jail. His objections were twofold. First, he was convinced that the jail was not an appropriate place for the mentally ill to be held— "never has been, never will be." In keeping with that philosophy, the director refused to pay for any mental health care out of the jail budget. Every organization that provided psychological services for inmates did so at its own expense or was subsidized by a third party.

The director's second objection to treating mentally ill prisoners at the jail stemmed from a fear that if he hired a psychologist, it would not be long before inmates began to take advantage of the person thus employed. "Pretty soon, everyone would need mental health services. The situation would mushroom out of control." The only treatment other than psychotropic medication that the director did allow at the jail was substance abuse counseling. AA conducted a meeting every Friday night, and the public health department had assigned an outreach counselor to work with a group of eight inmates for a total of 2 hours a week. The substance abuse unit at the mental health center was also willing to send staff members to the jail, but did not do so because the jail director was unwilling to help defray the unit's costs.

New inmates were screened by booking officers who had 40 hours of basic training and who attended in-service seminars sponsored by community mental health agencies. Floor deputies were also required to receive this training so that they could recognize inmates who exhibited symptoms of mental illness after intake. Emergency medical technicians supplemented the initial screening by conducting a brief medical exam to check each inmate's mental status. A prisoner facing serious felony charges would initially be placed in a special observation cell as a precaution against possible suicide attempts. An officer would then be assigned to monitor the individual every 15 minutes and make a note in a special log of what was observed.

Evaluations had formerly been conducted by an on-call psychiatrist, who was contacted whenever an inmate seemed to be in "desperate need." The practice had been changed 10 months prior to the site visit, when an inmate later diagnosed as psychotic nearly succeeded in killing himself. Jail officials realized that they would have been liable for damages if the prisoner had died, and had since called the crisis unit of the mental health center whenever it appeared that an inmate had a serious mental illness. In its first 10 months of operation, the crisis unit conducted 24 evaluations at the jail. However, inasmuch as the jail would not pay for the evaluations, a shift supervisor first had to request that the prisoner's attorney obtain a court order to have the inmate examined. The mental health center could then bill the court for any costs that were incurred. The jail administration liked this arrangement because it did not have to pay for the service and because the liability for a faulty diagnosis was transferred to another agency.

Inmates in need of inpatient care were sent to the state's single forensic unit. Meeting the legal admission criteria was a source of considerable frustration for correctional officials: "A guy must attempt to commit suicide about five times before the jail can get a court order for a 30-day evaluation. Sometimes it's a real fight, especially if the charges are minor." Once an inmate did cross the designated threshold, however, state law required that the hospital accept the patient immediately. Since space was very limited, nondangerous inmates were usually assigned to unlocked wards. Equally or perhaps even more troublesome from the jail's perspective was the fact that prisoners were sent back to the jail as soon as they were stabilized; inmates frequently returned after just a few days. In summary, this jail was concerned with identifying all possible serious problems—primarily because of liability issues—and then providing treatment only as needed and in limited amounts.

The Identification and Treatment Approach

Jails with an identification and treatment approach had not only identification services to help officers determine which inmates were mentally ill, but regular treatment services to help stabilize those who were in need of professional care. No arrangements were made, however, for the continuation of that treatment once an inmate was released.

Although medication and substance abuse counseling were frequently integral parts of an individual's overall treatment plan, they were not sufficient to warrant our designation as "treatment components" per se. Other treatment services, such as individual therapy and internal hospitalization, had to be available in order for a jail to be regarded as having regular, ongoing treatment in nonemergency situations.

Identification and treatment approaches generally sought to accomplish five principal goals: (1) to identify any inmates having serious or potentially serious mental health problems; (2) to monitor the condition of these inmates; (3) to stabilize mentally disturbed inmates in crisis situations; (4) to provide professional mental health care for disturbed inmates when it was realistic to do so; and (5) to transfer inmates to a psychiatric facility when inpatient care beyond that available at the jail was required. Treatment goals were typically immediate in nature— that is, to help an individual adapt to the conditions of confinement or to convince an inmate that suicide was not the answer to his or her problems.

When an inmate was admitted to a jail that had identification and treatment services, the identification process usually included an initial screening and some form of classification. Jail officials might not be able to treat all of the inmates found to be in need of nonemergency professional care, but at least a designated subgroup of these individuals would routinely be deemed eligible to receive those services that were available. The provision of treatment did not, of course, preclude the simultaneous use of one or more management techniques.

Urban Western Jail

A large Western jail that used the identification and treatment approach was located in a county covering approximately 8,000 square miles. Four hundred thousand residents resided permanently in the county, but the population more than doubled during certain parts of the year as the result of a heavy influx of tourists.

The jail had been built in 1960. Although it was still in fairly good condition, chronic overcrowding, lack of services, and poor administration had led to a class action lawsuit in 1977. An expert witness described it as the second worst that he had ever seen in the United States. In 1979, the sheriff had appointed a new administrator and signed a consent decree with 243 items addressing virtually every aspect of jail operation. The average daily population had since been reduced from 600 inmates to just over 250. The assistant director in charge of program planning noted that the limited availability of space was still a "great constraint" in his efforts to deliver high-quality mental health services. A new jail was under construction at the time of our site visit, however; this, he believed, would enable him to develop new program options.

The decree had a major impact on both the quality and extent of the jail's mental health services. One of the first things the new administrator did was to hire a private corporation to provide all health services. The contract called for the corporation to recruit additional medical and mental health staff members to work at the jail; to assume responsibility for the day-to-day management of service delivery; and to bring the facility into a state of compliance with those parts of the decree that concerned the inmate's health care. In February 1981, the jail was accredited by the AMA.

New prisoners were screened for signs of mental illness during intake by trained booking officers and received a brief

medical examination within 5 hours of admission. Those in
need of further evaluation were referred to the staff psychologist.
If an emergency arose when the psychologist was not available,
shift supervisors notified the crisis unit of the community mental health center, which had a psychiatrist on call 24 hours a
day.

According to the terms of the consent decree, suicidal inmates, the mentally ill, and any other prisoner whose adaptation to the general environment was "significantly impaired"
had to be referred for appropriate care. The decree further stipu-
lated that an individual treatment plan be developed for these
individuals by a physician or psychiatric professional, and that
a special classification process provide for their separate management and housing. Those who were ultimately determined
to be medium or high security risks are to be observed by a
correction officer at least every 30 minutes on an irregular schedule.

Outpatient treatment was provided in part by volunteers
from AA, who visited the jail once a week. The jail also had 13
nurses who distributed medication and looked after other inmate needs. The program administrator of health services estimated that nearly a third of all inmates received psychotropic
medication during 1980. She hoped to eventually replace much
of the medicine with behavioral therapy. The therapy that was
available at the time of our visit tended to be quite informal, but
the consent decree did call for at least one staff member to be
available for counseling inmates at all times.

Prisoners in need of inpatient psychiatric care were frequently
sent to the jail infirmary. Although none of the 25 beds were
routinely reserved for the mentally ill, there were usually at least
two or three inmates there for psychiatric reasons at any given
time. Inmates could also be sent to a separate locked ward within
a local hospital or to a state forensic unit. However, inadequate
security had been a problem at the hospital in the past, and the
forensic unit was 450 miles away. Jail officials used the forensic
unit primarily for inmates' competency examinations.

The changes introduced at this jail over the last few years
had reportedly improved the morale and attitude of both in-

mates and officers. The innovations were expensive to implement, but officials indicated that taxpayers did appear willing to assume the costs of the new services. Details of the lawsuit and its aftermath were extensively reported in the local press, which ultimately raised the level of public concern for the quality of jail operations.

Urban Northeastern Jail

A second jail where officials identified and treated mentally ill inmates was in a Northeastern state, in a county of just over 500,000 people. It was run by a county prison board, consisting of three county commissioners, the sheriff, the district attorney, a judge, and the county controller.

The jail had been built in 1884 and was in very poor condition at the time of our visit. According to ACA standards, each of the jail's 43 cells was only large enough to accommodate two inmates. The jail's population seldom fell below 170, however, so the correctional staff was forced to double the recommended occupancy. Plans for a new facility had been stalled by community disagreement as to where the jail should be located.

The county had what was generally considered to be one of the most firmly established and accepted community corrections programs in the country. There were fewer new inmates committed to the jail at the time of our visit than 5 years earlier, despite the fact that the county had the fastest-growing population in the state. Not surprisingly, local citizens were very supportive of efforts to help those who did get incarcerated. At the time of the site visit, 50 people were providing various inmate services at the jail on a regular basis without compensation. The jail's community service division was supervising 200 volunteers.

Incoming prisoners were screened by trained correction officers. As part of the process, the booking officer had to complete an emergency psychological checklist. An inmate would be given a full and immediate psychological evaluation if any question on this list was answered affirmatively. In addition, jail counselors interviewed all prisoners within 24 hours of admission. Both officers and counselors attended periodic in-service seminars organized by mental health staff.

The warden had made the development of internal treatment services a high priority for his administration. He believed that "having a forensic capability is as much a part of our program as security. In fact, it *is* security. Inmates with psychiatric problems are handled before they become security problems." Indicative of this orientation was the fact that the warden had ordered the director of treatment to act as the shift supervisor of correctional personnel whenever the regularly scheduled supervisor was sick or on vacation.

The cornerstone of the jail's mental health program was a $99,000 contract with a private agency. The agency had two components with separate staffing and budgets: a family court unit based at the county courthouse, and a correctional services unit headquartered at the jail. The correctional services unit had a four-part mandate: (1) to provide 24-hour emergency psychiatric care, (2) to conduct court-ordered pretrial evaluations, (3) to offer individual and group therapy, and (4) to consult with jail staff as the need arose. Providing these services were a PhD-level psychologist (32 hours a week), a psychiatrist (19 hours a week), two master's-level psychologists (10 and 16 hours a week), and a full-time office coordinator. The jail's director of treatment, who had a master's degree in human services, oversaw their work and acted as a liaison officer with custodial personnel. The jail also had two full-time and three part-time substance abuse counselors. Both individual therapy and group therapy were routinely available, and at the time of the site visit, social service staff were being trained to offer marital therapy as well. Twenty-five percent of all inmates received some form of therapy or adjustment counseling.

If a prisoner was in need of inpatient psychiatric care, a representative from the emergency and court services unit of the county department of mental health would be advised that a transfer was being considered. The representative would advise the inmate of his or her rights, complete the necessary paperwork, and contact the admitting physician at the state hospital. Local judges reportedly worked very closely with jail officials to facilitate the commitment process. Forty-six inmates were hospitalized during 1980. A local hospital was also willing to accept jail referrals, but the warden chose not to use it because security there was poor and because there were rarely any problems in getting inmates accepted for treatment at the state forensic unit. When a judge signed the prisoner's commitment order, he or she also signed a contempt-of-court citation that could be presented to the hospital administrator if the inmate was refused admission.

Of all the jails in the sample, this facility came the closest to constituting a mental health resource center for community agencies, in that nearly all psychological evaluations required by the county probation department, the public defender, and the district attorney's office were conducted at the jail. If the individual to be assessed had been released on bail, he or she was directed to report to the jail on the day that the tests were scheduled. The warden approved of this practice: "The jail should not be a warehouse. The current arrangement not only results in the maximum utilization of the jail staff's expertise, but does so in the most efficient manner possible." He did concede, however, that "the concept has gotten us into trouble. We're getting referrals to the jail for some people who have no business here. Some agencies think that we have better programs than are available on the outside." The director of the mental health agency that was contracted to provide services at the jail agreed: "Judges sometimes send people to jail just to get their recommendations."

The Comprehensive Approach

Jails offering a comprehensive range of mental health services both identified and treated mentally ill offenders during their incarceration; in addition, they referred those in need of ongoing care upon release to appropriate agencies in the community. Institutional responsibility for a prisoner's welfare was viewed in a somewhat broader context, in that the long-range interests of the individual were more explicitly taken into account.

The comprehensive service approach attempted (1) to identify any inmates having serious or potentially serious mental health problems; (2) to monitor the condition of these inmates; (3) to stabilize mentally disturbed inmates in crisis situations; (4) to provide professional mental health care for disturbed inmates when it was realistic to do so; (5) to transfer inmates to a psychiatric facility when inpatient care beyond that available at the jail was required; and (6) to link disturbed inmates about to be released with agencies capable of providing needed services in the community.

Day-to-day programming at jails with a comprehensive range of mental health services did not always differ dramatically from that found in jails where the mentally ill were identified and treated but were not referred for postconfinement care. The advantages and limitations of both types of programs were similar, and the quality of treatment might be as good at one type of jail as at the other. It was thus unlikely that facilities with a comprehensive range of services would vary significantly on many of the variables commonly used to measure a program's effectiveness or the extent of its impact within the jail. However, by routinely referring inmates whose release was imminent to community mental health agencies, a jail effectively forged a new link with the community mental health network. The continuity of professional care thereby became a goal for the jail as well as for the mental health system as a whole.

Metropolitan Southwestern Jail

A jail offering a comprehensive range of services was built in the Southwest in 1978 as the result of a court order issued 3 years earlier to reduce overcrowding. At the time of our site visit, it was operating within its rated capacity of 342 inmates, but was planning a 200-bed annex. The jail was operated by the city under a joint-powers agreement with the county. The chief administrator was appointed by the mayor in consultation with the county manager.

In fiscal year 1981, the jail allotted $162,000 for inpatient psychiatric services and emergency evaluations. This figure represented about 4.5% of the total jail budget. Responsibility for the delivery of mental health services was shared by two individuals: a social worker who supervised the provision of care for disturbed inmates in the general population, and a nurse who oversaw treatment on the psychiatric ward. Both they and their staffs were employed by a mental health center owned by the county but operated by the state university's school of medicine. The director of forensic services at the center viewed the jail as a legitimate component of a community-wide service network and believed that a jail client should have full access to all available care. The chief social worker was also pleased with the arrangement, believing that it resulted in the optimal use of university resources.

New inmates were screened by officers who not only received 80 hours of training in supervision and overall jail management when they were hired, but also received additional frequent (though irregular) in-service training organized by staff members from the psychiatric unit. Shortly after the prisoners were screened, they were given a medical exam by one of the jail's two nurses. Anyone found to be in need of a psychological evaluation was referred to a part-time PhD-level psychologist. Prisoners could also be brought to the mental health center for emergency assessments when the psychologist was not on duty. Competency exams were performed at a special clinic in the basement of the county court building.

Inmates needing treatment could be handled in several ways. Those with the most acute needs were taken to the psychiatric ward of a state prison if they were dangerous or required long-term care. The state forensic unit could be used, but jail officials preferred not to send prisoners there because it was 160 miles away. Inmates who did not pose a security risk could be treated at the mental health center's inpatient unit. Since the jail psychiatrist was employed by the mental health center, he was automatically granted admitting privileges. However, the most common method of dealing with inmates with acute mental health needs was to transfer them directly to the jail's 14-bed psychiatric unit. Space was sometimes problematic, but the infirmary would be expanded to 34 beds if the design of the proposed annex was ultimately accepted.

Partial hospitalization could be arranged for inmates with less serious impairments. When an inmate was discharged from the infirmary, he or she was frequently instructed to return to the unit three times a week for outpatient therapy. Social workers serving the general population also provided instruction in stress management and checked periodically for prisoners' problems. Two substance abuse counselors were available at the jail for consultation as well. Their primary role was to conduct assessments of pretrial inmates and to identify those who could benefit from transfer to a treatment program.

Mental health planning for an inmate's release began as soon as it was determined that the prisoner was in need of care. If the individual had been receiving help from a mental health agency prior to being arrested, a request was made for the person's therapist to visit the inmate if at all possible. A meeting was also scheduled between the therapist and relevant members of the jail mental health staff, so that arrangements for tentative referrals could be on file in the event of bail being met. The outside therapist was also asked to maintain regular contact with the inmate and to consult weekly with jail staff so that treatment and dispositional plans could be revised as necessary.

Inmates who were not receiving professional care at the time of their arrest received case management services from the mental health center's forensic liaison therapist. The therapist would assign a social worker from the center's outpatient unit to work with an inmate upon request from any member of the jail's psychiatric staff. This service was considered especially important if available resources did not permit an inmate to receive appropriate treatment while in custody, but the inmate could nevertheless benefit from specialized care.

Urban Far West Jail

A comprehensive range of mental health services had also been implemented at a local jail in the Far West. This facility was built in 1975 and had an average daily population of 65 inmates, 5 more than the building was designed to accommodate. The board of supervisors knew when they approved the plans for the new jail that 60 beds would probably be inadequate, in light of projected increases in the inmate population. They nevertheless voted to keep the facility small, because there was so much community interest in developing viable alternatives to incarceration. The board also decided to establish a department of corrections to operate the facility after a special task force concluded that past sheriffs frequently had neither the time nor the expertise needed to manage the jail in the most professional manner possible.

The administrator at the time of our site visit was a former deputy sheriff with a master's degree in special education. One of her major priorities has been "to meet the principal physical/social/mental needs of inmates so that prisoners can focus their attention on rehabilitation activities." This jail therefore, made a wide variety of educational and recreational programs available, in addition to extensive mental health services.

Efforts to identify new prisoners who were mentally ill were facilitated by the fact that new correction officers received 80 hours of state-mandated training when they were first hired. They received 24 hours of additional instruction each year thereafter. Both basic and in-service training included instruction in the recognition and management of the mentally ill.

Incoming prisoners were screened by the booking officer and were then examined by a registered nurse from the county health department. A six-person forensic team from the community mental health center also played a role in the identification process by meeting once a week to determine whether any of the new inmates had previously received professional care from center personnel.

The forensic team staff included a senior mental health worker, a mental health counselor, and a service coordinator, all of whom worked at the jail 20 hours a week. A drug counselor and alcohol counselor each contributed 10 hours weekly, and a psychiatrist participated in team activities for 4 hours a week. The team was formed shortly after the new jail opened, so that inmate care could be delivered more systematically than had previously been the case, when jail officials contacted individual service units at the center on an as-needed basis. Under the new arrangement, forensic team members conducted all nonemergency evaluations, met on a regular basis to discuss individual cases, and developed multifaceted treatment programs for inmates with multiple problems. Shift supervisors at the jail still called the crisis unit in emergencies.

The county employed private psychiatrists to conduct emergency exams as the need arose. However, the jail director was very dissatisfied with this approach. There was frequently a lapse of 1–2 months between the date when an exam was ordered and when it was finally conducted. Several more months might pass before the judge rendered a final decision on the issue.

The jail reported having little difficulty in transferring acutely ill inmates to the state hospital forensic unit, or, on occasion, to a prison hospital ward. Correctional authorities nevertheless sought to have an inmate hospitalized only as a last resort. The forensic team coordinator believed that even psychotics know right from wrong and that those who commit a crime belong in jail, not a mental institution: "When we hospitalize someone from the jail, correction staff feel like they have failed. We are not bleeding hearts. You act out, and we're locking your ass down."

A great deal of attention was thus given to the development of services within the jail so that hospitalization would not become necessary. Both the psychiatrist and the mental health counselor who served on the forensic team offered individual therapy, and the counselor conducted group therapy as well. Group and individual alcohol counseling were provided by a substance abuse specialist who came to the jail four times a week. Drug abusers could choose from counseling offered by Narcotics Anonymous, the Flower of the Dragon (an organization serving Vietnam veterans), and a staff member from the mental health center who led twice-weekly sessions. Support groups were also available for the general population. One such group provided "a supportive environment in which participants can air any subject of concern, e.g., the stress of incarceration, separation anxiety, depression, future goals, and substance abuse." Another group, limited to women inmates, confronted "issues unique to incarcerated women." About half of all inmates received some form of counseling.

Complementing the treatment component of the mental health program were the management and referral services provided by a "community resource team" that met twice a month. The team consisted of a correction officer, a nurse and a housing supervisor from the jail, two probation officers, a vocational rehabilitation specialist, a job developer, officials from the community justice program and mental health center, and a representative of two substance abuse organizations. The team reviewed the social and legal status of every inmate held for more than a few days at the jail and developed an action plan designed to help those in particular need of assistance. "Community justice volunteers," who were recruited by the jail to ease the inmates' transition into the community, also helped make appropriate community liaisons.

SUMMARY

Sorting out the types of mental health programs at the 43 jails studied produced what seemed to be four basic approaches. These approaches were distinguished both by the number and range of mental health services and by correctional and county officials' perceived obligations toward mentally disturbed inmates. To facilitate an understanding of what the jails were doing for their mentally ill inmates, the grouping of the 43 programs into the four major categories was considered useful.

Our major research concern, however, was not with a taxonomy of approaches to service delivery. Rather, our primary interest was in analyzing how these mental health programs were organized, in order to determine where the services were provided, who provided them, and how the jail administration linked up with the various providers of these services. Also, our concerns concentrated on whether any particular arrangement of mental health services was perceived to be more effective than any other, as well as on the extent to which the different arrangements of service produced (1) more or less conflict in the jail and (2) more or fewer problems of interagency coordination. Chapter 4 deals directly with these core questions.

Chapter 4

The Effectiveness of Jail Mental Health Programs: An Interorganizational Assessment

Chapter 3 has presented a descriptive profile of the mental health services for jail inmates that were available in the 43 study sites at the time of our initial fieldwork. Here, our focus shifts from the variety of jail mental health programs in these sites to a consideration of their organizational properties: who ran them, where they were located, and how the various components related to one another. The central question is whether the ways in which services were organized made any difference in how they operated and in their perceived effectiveness. We found in our fieldwork that mental health services for jail inmates could be provided under the auspices of both correctional and community mental health agencies, and that they could be provided within the jail or in external locations. The issue of greatest importance, from the perspective of program planning and development, is whether any particular combination of these organizational arrangements was more effective than another.

If the available data were to suggest that one organizational arrangement was clearly more effective, program planners in communities desiring to develop jail mental health services for jail inmates would have a single template to guide their efforts.

Alternatively, if the data were to suggest that no single organizational arrangement was superior to the others, then program planners must consider the benefits and costs associated with the choice of each organizational arrangement for their specific circumstances, such as jail size, the availability of mental health services in the local community, and the adequacy of program resources. At least, awareness of the problems associated with various ways of organizing jail mental health services can be expected to better inform local planning efforts.

INTERORGANIZATIONAL PERSPECTIVES ON SERVICE DELIVERY

Instead of viewing the jail as a self-contained or closed system, an interorganizational approach to program development and evaluation looks beyond the jail to its linkages with a variety of other organizations in its environment, such as state mental hospitals, psychiatric units in general hospitals, community mental health centers, and other health and human service agencies. The study of interorganizational relationships recognizes that interdependency is an important reality of organizational life and that organizations seek to manage such interdependency through both cooperative and competitive strategies (Thompson & McEwen, 1958; Warren, 1967; Warren, Bergunder, & Rose, 1974; Aldrich, 1979).

One specific focus of attention has been the area of interorganizational cooperation, wherein two or more organizations join together for the purpose of jointly accomplishing their individual operating goals. The structure and dynamics of such relationships have been examined in a variety of health and human service contexts (e.g., Aiken & Hage, 1968; Benson, Kunce, Thompson, & Allan, 1973; Warren *et al.*, 1974; Lehman, 1975; Whetten, 1977). In addition, a growing literature focuses on the larger community context within which organizations interact and environmental "contingencies" influence the level and course of interorganizational development (Whetten, 1977). As Schermerhorn (1975, p. 846) points out, "such an understanding is a necessary pre-condition for planned intervention and effective action." Moreover, this line of inquiry has called attention to the proposition that there is "no one best way" of designing interorganizational relationships (Perrow, 1970, p. 28). Different types of linkages can accomplish particular tasks and goals, and the appropriate structure and intensity of interorganizational relations will depend on contextual features of the environment as well as the characteristics of the interacting organizations (Morrissey, 1982b).

One promising approach for studying the interorganizational dimensions of jail mental health service programs can be found in the work of Newman and Price (1977a). In the course of a national study of drug treatment in local jails, they found that jails varied widely in the organization and scope of services provided to inmates. A typology reflecting this variability was developed to characterize four alternative organizational arrangements for service delivery: (1) an internal system, (2) an intersection system, (3) a linkage system, and (4) a combination system. These four systems were differentiated on the basis of administrative responsibility and the location of services.

In the internal system, a jail provides all inmate services from within its own organization, and interface with community-based agencies is minimal. The intersection system involves services provided by external human service organizations working cooperatively with the jail. Services are provided (by fee, by contract, or without charge) either by bringing staff into the jail or by transporting the inmates to the community agency. In the linkage system, one outside human service agency has direct contact with the jail. The linkage agency serves as an inmate case-finding and referral broker for the human services community. A combination system represents a mixture of two or more of the foregoing types. The jail interacts with several service providers, and two or more different sources (including jail staff, outside resources, and brokerage arrangements) provide services to inmates.

Consistent with the "no one best way" principle of interorganizational design, Newman and Price (1977a) suggest that distinct advantages and disadvantages may be associated with alternative service delivery arrangements for local jails. They note, for example, that coordination and security risks are minimized in an internal program when jail employees are the service providers, but the resource demands on the jail's budget are high, and problems may be encountered in hiring qualified employees. Programs based on linkages with external agencies, in contrast, reduce the demand on jail resources but heighten accountability and coordination problems with external agencies. Programs combining internal and external components are seen as the most complex type. They foster the greatest volume of services; however, they require a high level of resources from the jail as well as external agencies, they exacerbate coordination problems, and they run the greatest risk of duplication and discontinuity in service delivery.

The comparative advantages and disadvantages of these alternative service delivery arrangements, however, have yet to be empirically assessed. Newman and Price's (1977a) evaluations were based on qualitative information obtained largely from jail administrators and their staffs; no systematic survey of external human service agencies was undertaken in their study. Yet, to the extent that service delivery arrangements are dependent wholly or in part on community human service agencies, an interorganizational data base is required to evaluate the relative costs and benefits of each arrangement.

If differential costs and benefits are associated with alternative arrangements for delivering jail mental health services, a number of considerations have to be balanced in choosing an optimal program configuration for any given jail. Newman and Price (1977a) identified jail size, resource availability, and administrative efficiency as relevant considerations. Another crucial factor is the comparative effectiveness of each service delivery arrangement. In general, although issues of service outcome and clinical effectiveness must ultimately be evaluated through client-based epidemiological and experimental research (e.g., Attkisson, Hargreaves, Horowitz, & Soreson, 1978), studies of the perceived effectiveness of alternative service delivery arrangements can yield important insights for program planning and development.

Certain service delivery arrangements also may minimize
problems of interagency conflict, whereas others may exacerbate
them. Moreover, interagency conflict may also vary independently of perceived effectiveness. For example, programs that
experience high levels of conflict may still be viewed as highly
effective, whereas more placid programs may be seen as relatively ineffective by some observers or participating agencies.
Organizations, including jails, that attempt to mobilize available resources must coordinate activities with other agencies,
even in the richest of community environments. At the same
time, conflict is a near-ubiquitous feature of interorganizational
relations. Conflict may be particularly pronounced in arrangements such as those between jails and human service agencies,
which are often thought to have disparate goals and philoso-
phies with regard to inmate custody and rehabilitation. Quanti-
tative data on the prevalence and variation of these problems
can yield important information for assessing the costs and
benefits of each type of service delivery.

In view of these considerations, this chapter focuses on the
relationships between alternative interorganizational arrangements of jail mental health programs, their perceived levels of
interagency conflict, and their perceived effectiveness. As presented in Figure 4.1, our conceptual model for analyzing these
data consists of two parts: (1) the structural antecedents of perceived interagency conflict, and (2) the impact of conflict and
these structural variables on the perceived effectiveness of jail
mental health programs. The model suggests that interagency
conflict is a function of the administrative auspices and location
of a program, and that a program's effectiveness, in turn, is a
function of its auspices, location, and conflict.

MEASUREMENT

The data on program arrangements considered in this chapter
were gathered during our initial site visits to each of the 43 jail
mental health programs in 1981. Semistructured interviews were
conducted with sheriffs and jail administrators, mental health

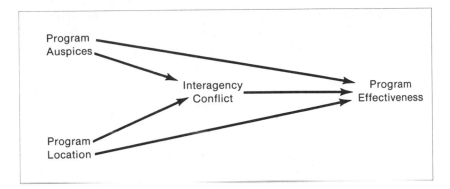

FIGURE 4.1. Interorganizational model for analyzing the effectiveness of jail mental health programs.

service chiefs within the jails (if any), staff members of external mental health agencies, and county executives or their designated spokespersons. These interviews provided the structural data on each jail (size, program auspices, and program location), plus other information about the availability of the inmate mental health services described in Chapter 3.

The data on perceived effectiveness, conflict, and coordination were obtained from a survey instrument mailed to all persons interviewed during the site visits, plus others these persons had nominated who were familiar with the jail and its mental health services. This questionnaire asked a series of closed-ended questions about the effectiveness of the local jail mental health program and the extent of conflict among participating agencies.

Our research staff developed perceived-effectiveness items on the basis of visits to three pilot sites in New York State; conflict items were adapted from a survey instrument developed by Van de Ven and his associates (Van de Ven & Ferry, 1980) to assess interorganizational relationships. The 584 forms that were mailed produced 398 responses (68%) from the 43 sites. No usable responses were returned from 1 site, reducing the total number of sites to 42. Of the respondents in these 42 sites, 138

(35%) were employed by jails, and 260 (65%) were affiliated with external mental health agencies. Four distinct staff groups were identified: members of jail mental health staffs ($n = 52$), members of jail correctional staffs ($n = 86$); members of community mental health center staffs ($n = 124$); and staff members in a variety of other organizations, such as state mental hospitals, general hospitals, and substance abuse agencies ($n = 136$).

A preliminary analysis of the program-level data indicated that the perceived-effectiveness items reflected two distinct components: (1) a range of safety goals, including the prevention of suicides and suicide attempts and the reduction of violence in the jails, and (2) a range of service goals, including the provision of appropriate and timely mental health care to jail inmates (Morrissey, Steadman, & Kilburn, 1983). Measures of the perceived effectiveness of programs in meeting each type of goal were constructed as summated scales from the component items. An analogous scale was constructed from two questionnaire items to measure levels of interagency conflict.

The administrative auspices and location of each jail mental health program were determined from information obtained during our site visits. Auspices were assessed in terms of the primary administrative control of mental health services (i.e., jail, external mental health agency, or a joint arrangement). Similarly, location was measured by the primary physical location of mental health services (i.e., within the jail, at an external agency, or some combination of the two). The distribution of the 42 jail programs across these two dimensions is displayed in Table 4.1.

The final variable included in the analysis was jail size. Size is a major determinant of variations in organizational structure (Hall, 1982). Moreover, our previous work, described earlier, suggested that certain types of mental health services, as well as program auspices and location, were related to jail size. Thus, to ascertain the effects of auspices and location on conflict and effectiveness, jail size was introduced as a control variable. The measure of jail size used here was the average daily inmate

TABLE 4.1. Distribution of Jail Mental Health Programs by Auspices and Location ($n = 42$)

Program auspices	Program location[a]			
	Inside jail	Outside jail	Combination	Total
Jail	4	0	0	4
Mental health agency	7	3	5	15
Joint auspices	12	0	11	23
Total	23	3	16	42

[a]The three empty cells were expected because they represent unlikely interorganizational arrangements. For example, a mental health program located entirely outside the jail, yet run by the jail, is quite implausible. Such programs would be run by an external agency, and, if so, they would be classified in another cell of the table.

population, which ranged in our sample of 42 jails from 19 to 630 (median size, 135).

INTERAGENCY CONFLICT

Results of our analysis only partially conformed to our conceptual model (Figure 4.1). When jail size was held constant, only program auspices seemed to affect the level of interagency conflict. Not surprisingly, perceived conflict was moderately high for programs operated under joint auspices. These arrangements entailed greater interdependence between jail staff and external agency staff in serving the needs of mentally ill inmates, and they presumably allowed disagreements to intrude in the service delivery process. In fact, intense levels of interorganizational conflicts were reported at sample sites, and many of the problems stemmed from circumstances specific to individual locations. Two of the more common types of disagreements concerned the optimal location for delivering services and the jail's lack of payment for services rendered.

Given the realities of severely limited transfer opportunities to state mental hospitals, correctional officials tended to prefer to

have as many services as possible provided at the jail, in order
to maximize security. Several administrators nevertheless agreed
to bring inmates to the mental health center for evaluations or
treatment because facilities at the jail were so antiquated. However, some officials indicated that they would do so only if a
correctional officer stayed with the prisoners at all times. Directors of mental health agencies generally believed that such an
arrangement would violate the principle of confidentiality. At
most of the sites where the sheriffs would not compromise on
this issue, the mental health centers ultimately yielded, but a
number of directors complained that the procedure required
twice as much staff time as would otherwise be the case. No
agreement could be reached in one county, however, with the
result that the shift supervisors asked a local ambulance service
to dispatch an emergency medical technician to the jail whenever an inmate needed a psychological evaluation.

The issue of payment was an even more sensitive topic. Few
jails had formal contracts with service providers to reimburse
them for the cost of delivering inmate care. Mental health centers at three locations billed the inmate/clients directly, but
none reported any success in actually collecting the fees. Most
agencies were thus forced to absorb all expenses themselves.
This was particularly annoying in those counties where the jails
were perceived as making unreasonable demands on limited
agency resources. The mental health center at one location
stopped doing evaluations for the jail altogether when the sheriff refused to use any discretionary funds to offset some of the
related costs. Overall, however, considerably less interorganizational conflict was reported than we had expected at the outset
of the study.

PROGRAM EFFECTIVENESS

The second part of our analysis focused on the perceived effectiveness of the 42 jail mental health programs. Effectiveness was
considered in relation to two distinct goals for these programs:
safety and service. At issue was the extent to which the conflict

and structural variables accounted for differences in the perceived effectiveness of achieving safety and service goals, regardless of jail size.

Safety Goals

Our analysis showed that, overall, respondents felt that the 42 jail mental health programs were moderately effective in meeting safety goals. However, programs considered to have a good deal of interagency conflict tended to be seen as ineffective in achieving safety goals.

Of the two structural variables, only program location explained some of the variation in achieving safety goals. Relative to programs located inside jails, those in outside or combination settings received significantly lower ratings on achieving safety goals. And, once the effects of interagency conflict and program location are considered, program auspices were found to have essentially no influence on perceived safety.

The absence of a significant effect for jail size indicated that the mental health programs were rated as uniformly effective in achieving their safety goals, regardless of the size of the inmate population. Only when there was much interagency conflict, and services were provided either in outside or combination locations, were programs rated as significantly less successful in attaining safety goals. Furthermore, the absence of a significant effect for program auspices suggested that safety goals were equally well met whether programs were operated by jail staff or by external mental health agencies. Thus, for safety goals, it would appear that the crucial structural factor was where the services are delivered, not which agency delivered them.

Service Goals

The results of this analysis showed that the study variables explained about half of the variation in the perceived effectiveness of programs in attaining service goals. Overall, the 42 jail mental health programs were considered only moderately successful in attaining service goals. Larger jails tended to be seen as less effective in achieving service goals than smaller jails, but the difference was not signifcant. Once the effects of jail size were controlled for, however, the perceived level of interagency conflict contributed substantially to perceived effectiveness in regard to service goals. For example, programs in which there was much interagency conflict were considered ineffective in achieving service goals. Also, programs run by mental health agencies declined in perceived effectiveness when they were located outside the jail.

These results only partially conformed to the proposed model. Other than the modest effect associated with small jails, perceived effectiveness in attaining service goals appeared to be related more to levels of conflict than to program location or program auspices. In other words, these findings suggest that mental health programs associated with smaller jails, as well as those with relatively low levels of perceived conflict, were more successful in attaining service goals. Under these circumstances, the volume of service delivery was rather low, and interagency relationships (when present) were relatively benign. Also, the likelihood was high that mentally ill inmates would be provided with an appropriate range of timely services and would be linked to external agencies when these were available in the community.

In summary, these results of our analyses revealed differential patterns of association between the measures of program structure and program effectiveness. Program auspices, for example, seemed to affect only the level of interagency conflict. Programs operated under joint auspices were perceived as having significantly higher levels of interagency conflict than those programs operated by mental health agencies alone. The extent of interagency conflict for jail-operated programs fell between these extremes. Program location was related only to the attainment of safety goals. Mental health programs located inside jails were perceived as more effective than those in combination or outside settings in achieving safety goals. Finally, with increases in perceived conflict, the effectiveness of both safety and service goals tended to decrease markedly.

COMPATIBILITY OF
SAFETY AND SERVICE GOALS

One of the more important findings that emerged from the foregoing analyses was a strong positive relationship between the two types of perceived effectiveness, indicating that jail mental health programs that were considered effective in attaining safety goals also tended to be seen as effective in attaining service goals. In short, it appeared that both goals were compatible and mutually supportive in these jail settings. This finding is notable, in light of prior sociological analyses of mental hospitals and correctional facilities, which suggest that therapy (service) and custodial (safety) goals are difficult to attain together in the same organization (Parsons, 1957; Costonis, 1966; Street, Vintner, & Perrow, 1966; Cormier, 1973).

At the time we initiated our perceived-effectiveness survey, our research interests focused more on macro-organizational design questions than on custody–therapy conflict issues in the local jail. Consequently, we did not ask respondents to comment on the frequency and scope of day-to-day conflict between correctional and mental health personnel working in our study jails. This issue became much more important as our research unfolded, and a separate survey was mounted to explore these issues. The results of this second survey are reported in Chapter 5, but we want to explore one aspect of the goal compatibility issue in more detail here.

The foregoing analyses were based on aggregated program-level measures of the programs' perceived effectiveness in attaining service and safety goals. Any differences in the extent to which each of the four staff groups (jail mental health staff, jail correctional staff, community mental health center staff, and staff in other mental health organizations) rated the compatibility of these goals would, therefore, have been averaged out. Accordingly, it is possible that the aggregated measures suppressed significant differences between the mental health staffs and correctional staffs involved in the delivery of mental health services to jail inmates. To determine whether such differences were present, we divided our program-level measures into separate scores for each of the four respondent groups.

The effectiveness of jail mental health programs in attaining safety goals was rated highest by the jail correctional staff, followed by community mental health center staff, jail treatment staff, and other mental health agency staff (hereafter referred to as "other" staff). These results indicated that the four staff groups were not uniform in their ratings. However, only the "other" staff differed significantly from the first three groups. The average ratings of jail correctional staff, jail treatment staff, and community mental health center staff did not differ significantly. This suggests that although these three groups agreed that the jails in our study attained safety goals quite effectively, "other" staff tended to rate the jails' achievement of safety goals much lower.

One interpretation of this finding relates to the differing involvement of the four staff groups in the day-to-day operations of jail mental health programs. Across the 42 study sites, respondents from the "other" staff group were less directly involved in providing services within the jail than were respondents from the other three groups. Respondents from these "other" agencies, as noted earlier, included forensic personnel from state mental hospitals, treatment personnel from local general hospitals, and a number of administrative or planning personnel from state and county mental health agencies. In general, these respondents were involved with jail inmates only in a segmental or indirect way (e.g., through off-site evaluations at local and state hospitals or through planning and administrative activities). Hence they tended to be less familiar with day-to-day programming and were undoubtedly less sensitive to the impact that mental health services had on inmate and staff behavior in the jails. In contrast, the three groups more directly involved in on-site service provision tended to concur that mental health services did enhance the attainment of safety goals.

With regard to the perceived effectiveness of jail mental health programs in achieving service goals, our results showed a similar lack of uniformity among the four respondent groups.

Community mental health center staff had the highest rating on service effectiveness, followed by jail treatment staff, jail correctional staff, and "other" staff. However, the only significant difference was between the community mental health center staff and the other three groups. This suggests that although the community mental health center staff felt that the jails in our study were quite effective in attaining service goals, the jail treatment staff, jail correctional staff, and "other" staff considered the success of these programs to be substantially lower.

Further insights into these effectiveness ratings were obtained by examining the differences between subgroup averages on safety and service goals. Overall, the average rating on safety goals was significantly higher than the average rating on service goals. This difference held for each of the respondent subgroups, although it was not statistically significant for community mental health center staff. In general, these comparisons indicate that respondents rated their jail mental health programs as more successful in attaining safety goals than in attaining service goals. Qualitative data obtained during our site visits suggested that this difference could be attributed, in part, to program priorities and the relative opportunities for accomplishing each goal in jail settings.

In setting program priorities, both correctional and mental health personnel tended to define safety goals as the first priority. In field interviews, when members of jail correctional staffs were asked to comment on the value of mental health services, they usually responded in terms of safety goals (e.g., reductions in suicide and violence). The administrator of a large urban jail in California, for example, told us: "We don't expect to cure [mentally ill inmates]. Our aim is to keep them safe so that they are no worse than when they came in here. . . . From an operations perspective, having mental health services in the jail has made a big difference by reducing assaults, suicides, sexual harassments, and arson." This response was fairly typical of correctional personnel, who described the value of mental health services in terms of "keeping the lid on" the jail and maintaining inmate security.

Mental health staff members also placed high priority on safety goals. In field interviews, they often acknowledged that traditional therapeutic goals involving long-term treatment and personality change were unrealistic for the most part in a jail setting. Because of overcrowding and the rapid turnover of inmates, jail treatment was oriented toward early identification, segregation from the general population, and crisis stabilization (usually involving psychotropic medication).

In terms of safety goals, then, there appeared to be a convergence of interest between correctional and mental health staffs. Such goals can be reasonably accomplished by providing adequate space for the segregation of mentally ill inmates and by having mental health personnel available for their care and supervision, either as part of the jail staff or from outside agencies. The relatively high ratings on safety goals suggest that the jail mental health programs included in this study were relatively successful in this regard.

Nevertheless, the ratings on service goals indicate that the jail mental health programs considered here were much less successful in getting inmates an appropriate range of services, outside hospitalization, or placement in community programs at release. Although these goals tended to be more central to the mental health staff than to the correctional staff, their accomplishment required resources beyond those that could be provided by the jails. Given the underfunding of community-based programs in most localities, there is little enthusiasm for programs that would preferentially funnel resources to jail inmates. In the public's view, the "worthiness" of jail inmates for special treatment is often questioned. This feeling is exacerbated by the reluctance of community general hospitals and other service agencies to develop programs for jail inmates, because they represent both a drain on scarce resources and a threat to the "integrity" of their services. Furthermore, the jail inmate is a county responsibility in most jurisdictions, and state agencies are often reluctant to assume this responsibility in the face of the revenue constraints and escalating costs associated with prisons and mental institutions. Thus, the discrepancy between accomplishing safety and service goals in jail mental health programs can be attributed in large part to the status of the wider community mental health service delivery system, rather than to differences intrinsic to the jail programs.

DISCUSSION

The findings presented in this chapter are consistent with those of previous studies in interorganizational relationships and point to a number of issues for further research. Overall, no single structural configuration of jail mental health programs achieved high ratings on the effectiveness of service and safety goals while also having low ratings on interagency conflict. Rather, a number of tradeoffs appeared to be associated with each interorganizational arrangement. A program that concentrated on the provision of services by mental health agencies to inmates outside the jail, for example, would seem to have reduced the level of interagency conflict, but the price appeared to be decreased effectiveness in attaining safety goals. In contrast, a program run by jail employees inside the jail would seem to have enhanced the attainment of safety goals, but the price appeared to be a higher level of interagency conflict when the jail did interact with outside agencies for mental health services. (Moreover, a program run inside the jail may not be a viable option for all communities. Internal programs make heavy demands on the jail's physical plant, specialized staff, and operating budget, and the inmate population must be large enough to justify the program expense [Newman & Price, 1977a].)

Programs that relied upon both internal and external components revealed yet another pattern of benefits and costs. By pooling scarce resources, those programs operated under joint auspices might expand the range of mental health services available to inmates while diminishing program costs to participating agencies. However, such arrangements appeared to promote high levels of interagency conflict, which, in turn, were associated with a decrease in the programs' perceived effectiveness in meeting safety and service goals.

Thus, what was suggested at the outset by the general interorganizational literature (Perrow, 1970; Whetten, 1977) is strongly supported by these findings: There is "no one best way" to organize jail mental health services. Our study has identified several contingencies that need to be considered in developing an optimal organizational arrangement for jail mental health programs, such as the availability of external mental health agencies, the auspices under which the program is operated, and the program's location. Moreover, the extent to which sponsors and participants are willing to tolerate interagency conflict and the extent to which such conflict is detrimental to jail operations are both crucial factors to be considered in designing programs.

Despite low overall levels of interagency conflict, our findings indicated that such conflict tended to increase when mental health services were provided under joint auspices within the jail. Because these arrangements called for the most intensive contact between correctional and mental health agency staffs, the resultant high levels of conflict supported arguments advanced by Hall, Clark, and Giordano (1978) that interorganizational conflict is a function of the intensity of relationships between agencies. Furthermore, our results on the compatibility of safety and service goals for local jail mental health programs appear to contradict the idea that these goals cannot be effectively attained together in local jail settings. (As noted earlier, however, we focused more directly on the question of day-to-day conflict between correctional and mental health personnel as part of our second survey of the 43 jail mental health programs, and a fuller assessment of these issues is presented in Chapter 5.)

On a practical level, our overall findings from this phase of the research highlight the dilemmas of mounting appropriate service arrangements for mentally ill persons in local jails. Although efforts to reduce the size of jail populations and to enhance mental health services located in jails might seem to be the best policy, the current fiscal distress of county and state governments may well preclude the level of appropriations necessary for their implementation (Janovsky, Scallet, & Jaskulski, 1982; Rawls, 1982a). Moreover, policies geared toward expanded linkages with existing community mental health agencies may founder on the resistance of these agencies to dealing with persons who are ostensibly "mad as well as bad." Lamb and Grant (1982), among others, have noted that the current system of voluntary community mental health care is inadequate for jail inmates, because they are extremely resistant to it. Effective strategies for dealing with this population may require new or hybrid institutional arrangements that offer treatment in a structured and protective environment. Short of such fundamental realignment in the roles and jurisdictions of the mental health and criminal justice systems, local jails will continue to be faced with the challenge of meeting inmates' mental health needs. Although formidable in their own right, these challenges are only a part of the broader problems of providing asylum and humane care for chronically mentally ill persons in the community (Turner & TenHoor, 1978; Talbott, 1981; Tessler & Goldman, 1982).

Although our findings illustrate the relevance of an interorganizational perspective for understanding the scope of these service delivery issues, our research on program effectiveness has only dealt with the perceptions of correctional and mental health personnel directly involved in a relatively small sample of jail mental health programs. Clearly, further research is needed to replicate these findings for a larger probability sample of local jails. Moreover, it would be extremely useful for program planning and evaluation purposes to design studies of the effectiveness of jail mental health services that are based on behavioral indicators of inmate outcomes. Such research would help to determine whether programs perceived as effective in meeting safety and service goals actually result in better client outcomes in terms of symptom stabilization, higher levels of community adjustment, and stable participation in community mental health services.

Nonetheless, the insights obtained from our current work underscore the fact that the way in which jail mental health services are organized does make a difference in the ways in which such programs are evaluated by both mental health and correctional personnel. Knowledge of the tradeoffs involved in different arrangements of program auspices and location can make local planners aware of the problems likely to emerge under each arrangement. To the extent that such problems can be anticipated from the outset, corrective or preventative measures might be developed to forestall, mitigate, or avoid them.

_____

Chapter 5.

Scope and Frequency of Conflict Between Mental Health and Correctional Staffs

Our attention shifts in this chapter to the scope and frequency of day-to-day conflicts between correctional and mental health personnel in our sample of 43 jails. The results of our perceived-effectiveness survey, reported in Chapter 4, suggested that safety and service goals were highly compatible in the jail mental health programs we studied. However, we acknowledged that more direct measures of differences emanating from potential therapy–custody conflict were needed to fully answer questions about the compatibility of mental health and correctional personnel in local jails.

When our research began, we had no intention of focusing on internal staff conflict. Our frame of reference was an interorganizational one. However, as the site visits to the 43 jails progressed, we were continually struck by the frequency with which correctional personnel—both administrators and front-line officers—commented that the mental health personnel had made their job easier. On the other side, although mental health staff members often complained about trying to do their job in a jail, they also felt an overriding satisfaction in providing needed services in a receptive environment. Because of the discrepancies between our initial expectations on these issues and our on-site impressions, we developed a questionnaire on sources of conflict in the day-to-day operations of jail mental health programs; this was mailed to most of the jail and mental health staff members about 18 months after the original site visits. The results of these questionnaires reinforced our fieldwork impressions and the organization-level findings reported in Chapter 4. Both sources of data contrasted sharply with the ideas found in prior discussions about the delivery of mental health services in correctional settings.

PRIOR RESEARCH ON CUSTODY-THERAPY CONFLICT

It has become almost axiomatic in sociological analyses of interactions between mental health and criminal justice personnel to assume that their respective ideologies are inherently contradictory. The pervasiveness and immutability of conflicts between the rehabilitation and custody orientations are usually viewed as detrimental to effective mental health services in correctional settings. The classic statement of such conflicts facing mental health professionals in the criminal justice system is perhaps that of Powelson and Bendix (1951):

> The only professional group which comes into the prison for positive reasons is that of the custodial employees. They enter the prison with the clear objective of punishing convicted offenders and protecting society. Perhaps members of the other professions (doctors, psychologists, teachers, vocational counselors, and many others) enter the prison for equally clear reasons, for instance, to promote the rehabilitation and the health of prisoners. Yet, they cannot, in fact, pursue this goal. . . . Custody looks at the activities of the other divisions as evidence of misguided humanitarianism. It will tolerate them only after it is satisfied that every conceivable breach of security and discipline has been guarded against. The guards suspect the other divisions of being "soft." (pp. 77–78)

This perception of clashing ideologies that produce enduring conflict between correctional and mental health staffs in prisons has been supported in a number of papers (Cormier,

1973; Cumming & Solway, 1973; Kaufman, 1973; Roth, 1980) and empirically documented in juvenile detention facilities (Zald, 1963; Street *et al.*, 1966; Perrow, 1966). Also, a parallel theme of custody–therapy conflict emerging from sociological analyses of state mental hospitals (Parsons, 1957; Perrow, 1965; Costonis, 1966; Steadman, Cocozza, & Lee, 1978) is that such facilities have a dual nature: manifest treatment aspirations coupled with latent social control functions.

Both the sociological analyses of state mental hospitals and the research on the delivery of mental health services in correctional settings strongly suggest that, because of technological imperatives, custody and control functions routinely tend to displace therapeutic goals in dual-mandate organizations. Since the technology of custody far outstrips that of treatment, and since outcomes are so much more easily measured for custody than for treatment, it is assumed that custody considerations inevitably predominate whenever a facility has these dual mandates. As Costonis (1966) noted, "Custodialism depends upon a simple policy of containment which is relatively easy to implement and to measure. Treatment, on the other hand, places the issues of evaluation back into the problems of type and kind of therapeutic practices and the difficulties of measurement" (p. 81).

Since the applicability of these custody–therapy analyses of state prisons, juvenile detention facilities, and state mental hospitals to local jails had not been determined prior to the outset of our research, we had little to suggest that things might be different in jails. In fact, the correctional literature, without specifying any particular type of facility, argues the thesis that "conflict between custodial and professional staffs is one of the major administrative problems in the field of corrections" (Culbertson, 1977, p. 28). Yet our informal interview data indicated very little conflict in the basic goals of correctional and mental health staffs among our sampled jails.

The similarity of correctional workers' and mental health workers' viewpoints that were heard on our site visits is evident in the following responses from an administrator of a large urban jail and the director of a mental health unit in another large urban jail concerning the value of jail mental health services:

> We don't expect to cure [mentally ill inmates]. Our aim is to keep them safe so that they are no worse than when they came in here. . . . From an operations perspective, having mental health services in the jail has made a big difference by reducing assaults, suicides, sexual harassments, and arson.

> We just don't have the luxury of long-term therapy here. Mental health services for this population need to be quick, effective, and appropriate. We try to encourage medications and to stabilize them quickly. After they are settled and quiet, we can then focus on discharge plans . . . either getting them back into the general population or into an outside hospital or some other appropriate program.

Despite the number of times we heard such views, we remained skeptical, given the consistency of the sociological and correctional literature on these issues. One explanation we considered was that an interorganizational perspective and our interview schedules were not sufficiently sensitive to these types of conflicts. Furthermore, it was possible that on ideological grounds mental health and correctional staffs had little conflict, but that in day-to-day interactions there was substantial conflict. Such a distinction would be consistent with Pondy's (1969) distinction between "frictional conflict," which is relatively minor and does not alter the organizational structure, and "strategic conflict," which is deliberately created to permit weak members to force powerful members to relinquish control. Since strategic conflict is not crucial to our analysis, we wish to distinguish between "frictional conflict" and "goal conflict," as discussed in Chapter 4 with reference to safety and service goals.

As previously noted, our site visits and the interorganizational measures demonstrated surprisingly little conflict on fundamental goals between mental health and correctional staffs. Both groups were committed to keeping the inmates safe from themselves and one another, as well as to protecting staff from bizarre and assaultive inmates. As one district attorney observed, "The goal of the jail [correctional] staff is to 'keep 'em safe.' The mental health services need to be quick, effective, and appropriate. They need to prevent deterioration and injury to self or others." This view is entirely consistent with that of the jail psychologist who said that "the treatment goal of our mental health program is to get them to adjust to being incarcerated."

The consensus that seemed to exist on basic mental health goals left untouched the question of whether substantial frictional conflict might exist in the day-to-day operation of the jail. Previous sociological analyses of custody–therapy conflict have not found such a distinction necessary for the organizations examined. In the prisons, juvenile detention facilities, and even state mental hospitals of the 1950s and 1960s, the custodial and therapeutic ideologies were so sharply divergent that conflict was inherent. Powelson and Bendix (1951) even asserted that "the prison psychiatrist must come into conflict with the custodial treatment of prisoners if he follows the precepts of his profession" (p. 80). This situation, however, may be quite different for jails in the 1980s. If this were found to be the case, not only would some refinement of the custody–therapy concept in future analyses be suggested; the frequent pessimism from the fields of psychiatry and psychology about the ability of mental health services to provide effective services in correctional facilities would also be challenged.

Our research approach to these questions involved a mail survey of mental health and correctional staffs in the 43 jail mental health programs. The survey instrument was composed of 23 statements designed to tap a range of conflicts that might occur in a jail with an ongoing mental health program. The items were developed from site visits and interviews with mental health and correctional staffs. The individual items were factor-analyzed to produce two frictional-conflict scales; the relationships of these scales to a number of organizational and staff characteristics of each jail mental health program were then examined. Ultimately, the relationships of staff characteristics to levels of conflict suggested that a distinction between frictional and goal conflict was important for an accurate depiction of custody–therapy relationships in correctional mental health settings.

MEASUREMENT

In order to obtain a more direct measure of the frictional conflict in these programs, a survey instrument was pilot-tested, revised, and mailed in early 1982 to those persons who responded to the original survey at the 43 jails. Initially, 345 questionnaires were mailed to those persons directly involved in the jail mental health services; this produced a response rate of 51%. Two follow-ups increased the final response rate to 67% (232 total respondents). This sample was more closely targeted than that for the perceived-effectiveness survey discussed in Chapter 4, since the types of conflict of interest here were limited to circumstances in which mental health and correctional staffs directly interacted.

Although responses were anonymous, it was possible to identify the jail program with which a respondent was affiliated. From this information, it was determined that the respondent sample was unbiased. A breakdown in jail size, program location, and program auspices yielded only one significant difference between the respondent and nonrespondent groups. More respondents than nonrespondents were from small jails (18% and 7%, respectively), but small jails were slighty underrepresented initially, so no major problem of interpretation was apparent.

The eight-page questionnaire focused on a variety of areas, but for our purposes the core items were 23 questions focusing on specific day-to-day issues that might be sources of conflict between correctional and mental health staffs. The questions inquired about such things as "mental health staff's access to inmates," "inmates being placed on the mental health tier without mental health staff approval," and "recommendations of mental health staff being overridden by security staff," among others. The items were developed from site visits to two non-sample jails and from a pilot test of an earlier version of the questionnaire with correctional and mental health staffs at one of these jails. In order to insure confidentiality and maximize candid responses, the only items of identifying information sought were the name of the jail, the respondent's position, and the respondent's employer.

Upon initial examination, the 23 items were factor-analyzed to reduce the number of dependent measures of conflict. Two factors were found to account for 32% of the variance, and additive scales were created for both factors. The first scale, labeled "Treatment Conflict," was comprised of five items that addressed conflict in the day-to-day delivery of mental health services in the jails. The items were (1) access to mentally ill inmates; (2) mental health staff encountering delays in getting around the jail; (3) mental health staff's recommendations being overridden by security staff; (4) mental health staff's recommendations not being followed up by correctional officers; and (5) resistance to the transfer of mentally ill inmates to special housing units.

Several examples of treatment-related conflict were observed during the site visits. Counselors in a substance abuse agency at one site stated that their regularly scheduled weekly meetings with inmates were frequently canceled at the last minute because there were reportedly not enough deputies on duty to provide adequate security in the area of the jail reserved for programming activities. Mental health center personnel at another site reported considerable irritation over the fact that when they responded to the jail's requests for assistance, the shift supervisor would often forget to advise the officer controlling admission to the jail that such a request had been made. A center psychologist would then have to stand for several minutes in a small waiting area while the officer obtained authorization to let him or her enter. A related, albeit distinct, source of friction at many locations was the insistence of correction officers that mental health center personnel go through a metal detector and have their briefcases searched every time they went to the jail. Mental health personnel felt that this procedure constituted a needless delay and inconvenience, especially since they had already demonstrated their trustworthiness on security matters during numerous prior visits.

The second scale, which we called "Role Conflict," seemed to tap some type of role infringement, as measured by items such as the following: (1) mental health staff requesting privileges that ran counter to established jail procedures; (2) pampering of inmates; (3) getting involved in jail business; and (4) correction officers requesting mental health records inappropriately. This type of conflict was evident among two employees of a community mental health center in a large county in the South. One of the individuals was a PhD-level psychologist who had been assigned to work at the jail on a full-time basis by the center's court services unit. His official responsibilities consisted primarily of conducting evaluations and facilitating the transfer of psychotic inmates to inpatient facilities, although he also prescribed psychotropic medication in cases of emergency. He was able to do so because the jail physician had given him a number of signed but otherwise blank prescription forms to use when the doctor could not be located. A psychiatrist from the adult outpatient unit of the mental health center learned of the practice as a result of his occasional consultations at the jail, and openly condemned it as being unethical, illegal, and potentially quite dangerous. The psychologist, in turn, saw the psychiatrist as basically inept and out of touch with many of the more pressing needs of jail administrators.

As in Chapter 4, the independent variables examined were program auspices, program location, size of jail inmate population, and respondents' profession and agency affiliation. "Auspices" referred to the agency that had primary administrative control of the services (the jail, an external mental health agency, or a joint arrangement). "Location" referred to the actual location of the jail mental health program (inside the jail, outside the jail, or a combination of the two). "Size" was the average daily census in the jail (jail populations were classified as small, medium, or large). Respondents' profession was indexed by their actual position or job title at the time of the survey; we used seven categories of various correctional and mental health positions (sheriff or deputy, psychiatrist or other MD, mental health administrator, nurse, psychologist, social worker, and other mental health therapist). "Affiliation" referred to a respondent's employer, which in most cases was either the jail, a county mental health agency, or another mental health agency.

ISSUES PRODUCING STAFF CONFLICT

As indicated in our earlier field interviews, there was a relatively low level of frictional conflict for both mental health and correctional staffs on both the Treatment Conflict and Role Conflict scales. The only significant effects of any of the independent variables on either of the two conflict scales were those of respondents' profession and affiliation on Treatment Conflict. The Role Conflict scale was not significantly associated with any of the predictor variables.

An examination of the organizational variables produced a few additional significant findings. With regard to jail size, it was found that size alone was not significant in accounting for differences in the Treatment Conflict variable. However, for those programs located in the jail, there was a significant difference in the amount of treatment conflict between small and medium-sized jails. In these internal programs, staff in small jails perceived a far lower level of conflict than did staff in the medium-sized jails. Overall, staff in medium-sized jails had the highest score on the Treatment Conflict scale, followed by those in large jails, with the lowest score in the small jails; however, this difference was not significant.

The profession and affiliation variables were considerably more important than organizational variables. The relationship between the Treatment Conflict scale and respondents' position was found to be significant. The "other mental health therapist" category showed the highest amount of treatment conflict, while the lowest level was perceived by sheriffs and deputies. To collapse the categories and make the position variable more interpretable, an analysis of variance was done that broke respondents' position down into three categories: jail staff, medical mental health staff, and nonmedical mental health staff. This categorization also yielded significant results. Nevertheless, from our pilot interviewing, we felt that it might be more important to distinguish between treatment personnel employed by the jail and those employed by other mental health agencies.

Analysis of the affiliation variable (jail, county mental health agency, other mental health agency) suggested that each of these three groups was significantly different from the other two. The groups employed by the jail scored lowest on the Treatment Conflict scale, followed by those employed by the county mental health agency. The highest level of treatment conflict was perceived by the "other mental health agency" group, which was composed primarily of drug and alcohol counseling agencies and some state mental health personnel. Although this difference was statistically significant, we still felt that there might be important substantive distinctions between jail correctional staffs and jail mental health staffs. If, in fact, the previously discussed custody–therapy differences were at all applicable to the situation in local jails, the highest conflict could perhaps be expected among those mental health personnel who worked full-time inside the jail.

The variables created to test this possibility was comprised of four staff categories: jail correctional personnel, jail mental health personnel, county mental health personnel, and other mental health personnel. Once again, results with the Role Conflict scale were not significant. However, this staff categorization *was* highly significant in explaining differences in the Treatment Conflict variable. This was to be expected, given the previous separate analyses of the effects of position and affiliation. The reported means for the four groups demonstrated that the jail correctional staff perceived the lowest level of conflict in providing treatment to jail inmates. The jail mental health and county mental health staffs reported an equal and slightly higher amount of conflict. The most substantial difference was between other mental health agency personnel and correctional personnel.

These results, showing occupational differences in the amount of conflict perceived by correctional and mental health staffs, suggested the presence of frictional conflict that was not evident when the focus was on more generic goal conflict. These frictional conflicts were less consequential for accomplishing organizational goals than goal conflicts, and they did vary by type of mental health staff. According to these results, it appears that prior discussions of custody–therapy issues did not achieve the level of specificity that the local jail of the 1980s apparently requires.

DISCUSSION

Two major empirical conclusions have emerged from these analyses of day-to-day conflict in the delivery of mental health services in local jails. First, we found that the overall level of conflict in mental health service programs for this type of correctional facility was less than would be suggested by the sociological literature on prisons and state mental hospitals. Second, there were differences in the amount of conflict reported by security staff and mental health staff that were not found when conflict measures focused on organizational goals. From these empirical conclusions, a number of practical and substantive implications follow.

When staff members in jails that had ongoing mental health programs were asked about day-to-day conflict between the custodial and therapeutic staffs, the amount they reported was quite low. This may at least in part be attributable to the fact that jails have a correctional mission very different from that of prisons, and one that is less divergent from mental health goals than the mission of prisons. In contrast to prisons, which are long-stay institutions, U.S. jails in 1982 reported that the average length of an inmate's stay was 11 days (Bureau of Justice Statistics, 1983). Especially in terms of safety goals, there is a convergence of interest between correctional and mental health staffs in local jails. The goal of reducing inmates' violence toward themselves and others can be reasonably accomplished in most jails by providing adequate space for the segregation of mentally ill inmates, by having mental health personnel (who are either part of the jail staff or from outside agencies) available for their care and supervision, and by dispensing psychotropic medication. Moreover, the relatively high effectiveness ratings on safety goals reported in Chapter 4 indicate that jail mental health programs are able to accomplish these objectives with minimal custody–therapy conflict. As such, there is little support here for the thesis that correctional and mental health staffs in jails operate from fundamentally opposite and antagonistic perspectives. Although the mental health personnel we surveyed tended to be annoyed when their services were defined as a means to the end of secure custody, they nevertheless placed a high priority on safety goals.

The objectives of keeping themselves safe from violent inmates and keeping inmates safe from themselves and from other inmates are uppermost in the minds of the custodial personnel. In many instances, mental health professionals can clearly contribute to these goals. In doing so, these professionals practice their craft of crisis intervention and stabilization in ways that protect both the inmates under treatment and other persons in the jail. Accordingly, the ideological conflicts that might be expected where mental health efforts seek major personality changes are not present. These latter goals may be more typical of those correctional institutions (prisons and juvenile detention facilities) where earlier analyses of the custody–therapy conflict were conducted.

Nonetheless, while there were few apparent conflicts in goals between custodial and therapeutic staffs in the local jails we studied, there were some areas involving day-to-day procedures in which conflict did exist. We have suggested that Pondy's (1969) concept of frictional conflict accurately describes issues in these areas. This distinction between more generic organizational goals (or strategies that may involve reallocation of resources to achieve these goals) and more mundane sources of conflict is significant in refining sociological conceptualizations of custody–therapy conflicts in organizations with these dual mandates. It is thus inadequate to take at face value what appear to be two conflicting paradigms. In fact, in certain types of organizations, such as the local jail, the goals of custody and therapy converge. The primary purpose of both is to keep clients safe—from themselves, from other inmates, and from the correctional staff.

The convergence of goals in this instance appears to be related to two factors: (1) jails are involved in short-term "people processing," and (2) the technology of mental health treatment for this short-term organizational mandate is more developed than that for longer-term mental health treatment goals, or "people changing." The main mission of the local jail is to deliver these people, as one respondent noted, "no worse than when they came in here" to the court for arraignment, pretrial hearings, adjudication, or sentencing. A secondary function of local jails in most states is to house persons sentenced to stays of less than 1 year. The jail is a very high-turnover organization. Because of this, the mental health treatment staff cannot get involved in long-term therapy. Treatment in a jail is primarily a matter of stabilizing highly agitated or severely depressed persons who present high risks of committing suicide or attacking other inmates or jail staff. Stabilization in these acute situations occurs quite dramatically, through psychotropic medications and segregation from the general population. In some instances, there are efforts to counsel the inmates or to refer them to services in the community when these exist. Long-term therapies geared to major personality changes—the types of therapies that characterize "people-changing" organizations (Hasenfeld, 1972)—are rarely attempted. Because rehabilitation in the traditional sense is a minor goal for jail mental health personnel, who are more concerned with crisis stabilization, basis ideological conflicts with correctional personnel are infrequent and occur much less often than frictional conflicts.

Obviously, the technologies for these short-term mental health goals are quite well developed, not unlike the technologies of custody. Thus, in the instance of mental health services for local jails, the conflicts that may be produced by the huge ascendancy of one type of technology (custody) over the other (therapy) are diminished greatly. As a result, there is less conflict in the sphere of ideology and organizational goals. Nonetheless, frictional conflict, which is found in any organization, does exist. Thus, discussions with jail personnel will elicit complaints about conflict between the custodial and mental health staffs, but the conflict does not produce an antipathy that precludes attainment of the mutual goals of both staffs.

We do not mean to say that other approaches to mental health treatment, if employed in the jail, would not generate considerable conflict. As one psychologist noted, "There is little conflict because nothing is being contested. If mental health professionals tried to do real treatment, then real conflict might develop. The jail recognizes this and recruits accordingly. There are mental health professionals who can't work in the jail." Reinforcing this same point, an administrator in another jail said, "To the extent that mental health staff are seen as managing the inmate, conflict will be less. We are all doing the same thing. The front-line officer sees the mental health staff as 'helping me to do my job better.'" Consequently, as a psychologist aptly put it, "Very rarely do we come into conflict about goals, especially safety and management, [although we do] sometimes about means."

The bottom line for many mental health professionals in this environment is to view the jail itself as the client, instead of the individual inmate. To the extent that some crisis intervention or regular prescription for psychotropic medication keeps an inmate calm and quiet, the inmate is better off, and so too is the entire closed environment of the jail. If individual treatment were more ambitious, much more therapy in the form of individual counseling and group sessions would become more pervasive, and conflict, as well as service costs, would probably increase dramatically. However, given the nature of the jail, such treatment goals are unrealistic, while safety management needs are acute. As a result, mental health professionals who are willing to work toward less traditional treatment goals can function within the jail with minimal goal conflict.

The results reported here suggest that greater specification is needed in custody–therapy analyses to distinguish between various types of conflict that occur, and to acknowledge that custodial and therapeutic goals converge in certain types of organizations in ways that permit both types of staffs to achieve their respective goals ethically. These issues appear to warrant new research initiatives. Not only are there additional organizations in which the custody-therapy ideas require testing, but also the facilities and technologies of the 1980s are not those of 20 or 30 years ago, when the seminal studies in this area were conducted. These are issues of practical and substantive importance that merit renewed empirical investigation.

Chapter 6

Factors Contributing to the Survival and Development of Jail Mental Health Programs

The fourth major question of our research was that of how well the 43 study jails fared over the period of our project. Given the vast array of external pressures to upgrade services and the tremendous fiscal burdens being shifted to localities during a time of severe economic recession, it was uncertain how these jails would survive. Again, it should be noted that this jail sample was not representative of all U.S. jails with mental health programs. The 33 sites that had sent representatives to the 1979 NIC workshops on jail mental health services and the 10 supplemental sites were selected for study because they already had, or soon were expected to have, better-than-average mental health programs. Thus, the research focused at this stage on what staying power these programs had within fiscally restraining environments.

It was clear from our initial site visits that mental health programming at many sites was still in a state of transition. Four jails were under court orders or consent decrees to improve the quality of inmate psychiatric services. Similar suits had been threatened or were actually being prepared at several other locations. Even those officials who felt reasonably secure from the threat of a class action suit frequently expressed concern about the possibility that the family of a disturbed prisoner might seek compensatory damages in court if jail staff failed to detect and treat a serious mental ailment in a timely manner.

To assess changes in the 43 jail mental health programs, our research staff telephoned officials at the sample jails during a 3-week period in the fall of 1982. The length of time between the original site visits and the follow-up survey varied from 15 to 20 months. Three telephone interview schedules were developed to tap (1) broad administrative developments, such as changes in the average daily population and in the facility's budget; (2) specific modifications for mental health services at the jail, such as staff turnover, changes in the need for psychiatric care, and any problems that were reportedly interfering with the effective delivery of services at the time of our original site visits; and (3) changes in the organizational environment that might have had a direct or indirect impact upon the mental health program at the jail, such as the emergence of a prisoners'-rights group, the election of a new county executive, new diversion programs, mandatory sentencing laws, or internal policy changes at county mental health agencies.

At 16 of the 43 sample jails (37%), one jail official answered all the questions. These jails were typically very small and did not have any full-time medical or mental health staff members. Two individuals were contacted at each of the remaining 27 sites. The sheriff or a designated spokesperson answered the first series of questions about administrative changes, and the person most responsible for mental health services was asked about substantive programmatic developments. Both were asked about the organizational environment. A total of 70 people were interviewed, and nearly 250 phone calls were required.

CHANGES IN STAFF AND SERVICE PROVIDERS

One of the prerequisites for program development is the employment of qualified staff members who can both plan and implement necessary changes. Turnover of key personnel is thus a critical variable. It may have a very positive impact when staff members who have burned out or who are not performing effectively are finally replaced, or it may greatly complicate the goal of providing inmates with good-quality psychiatric care.

It is important to note that mental health services in jail settings may be influenced by the turnover of personnel in a number of roles besides those of psychiatrist, psychologist, and social worker. Nurses, for example, usually distribute medication and monitor the condition of psychiatric cases confined to the jail infirmary. Doctors may be called upon to evaluate prisoners who have been behaving in a strange manner. In the smaller jails, even correction officers may be expected to help classify inmates and contact the mental health center when the need arises.

During our original site visits, 50 corrections officers were identified as being directly involved in the delivery of mental health services. Of these, 5 (10%) had left prior to the follow-up. No data could be found for comparison purposes on the turnover of jail officers nationally, but it may be worth noting that custodial personnel in state prisons reportedly have an annual turnover rate of 20% (Lunden, 1965). In any event, the vast majority of custodial officers who arranged or otherwise provided inmate mental health care retained their jobs during the period under study. Since 38 sites (88%) were unaffected by any such shift in custodial personnel, we might reasonably conclude that this type of turnover had a minimal influence on programming changes.

Turnover of medical and mental health staff was far more problematic. A list of 263 people who had provided psychiatric services to jail inmates at the time of our site visits was compiled. Administrators contacted during the second round of data collection were able to confirm the employment status of 239 (91%). Of the 239 medical and mental health personnel confirmed, 67 (28%) no longer served jail inmates. This proportion is comparable to the 30% annual turnover rate for social workers in state and local welfare organizations (U.S. Children's Bureau, 1965) and the 28% rate often cited for nurses (Prestholdt, *et al.*, 1970; Tierney & Wright, 1973). Nevertheless, it is still more than twice the 13% median turnover rate found in nonprofit organizations for professional and technical workers generally (Price, 1977).

Small jails (average daily population of 50 or less) experienced the least turnover. Only 7% of the mental health staff who worked in such facilities had left. Medium-sized jails (average daily population of 51–250 inmates) had a 28% turnover rate, while 38% of the medical and mental health staff had left the large jails. One of the reasons why the smaller jails experienced the least turnover was that most mental health professionals assisting these facilities did so on an as-needed basis, and those who worked part-time in the jails were much more likely, as a group, to have kept their positions. Of the 239 staff whose status was verified, 176 (74%) were part-time jail employees. Of these, 37 (21%) had left. By contrast, of the remaining 63 individuals who worked full-time with inmates, 31 or nearly half (49%) were no longer there at the time of the follow-up. This result raises the possibility that burnout may be a serious problem among those whose work involves prolonged daily contact with mentally ill inmates.

A second reason why the smaller jails experienced less turnover was related to the occupational stability of the person most responsible for mental health services and the subsequent effect of this stability on subordinates. The top mental health administrator retained his or her position at all of the 8 small jails, at 15 of the 22 medium-sized jails (68%), and at 7 of the 13 large jails (54%). The larger the jail, the more likely the administrator was to have been replaced. The implications of such a development can be seen in Table 6.1. At facilities where a new chief of jail mental health services had been hired, turnover was 2½ times greater than that in jails where the director had retained his or her position. And turnover was greater regardless of administrative auspices or the amount of time personnel spent with inmates.

An interesting observation on how staff turnover may be a problem was offered by a jail administrator during one of our site visits. He observed that for individual inmates during their stays in jail, staff turnover was no problem because the stays were typically so brief: "Inmates don't see turnover. From their perspective, turnover is irrelevant. It is a problem only from the administrative standpoint." Staff turnover thus became prob-

TABLE 6.1. Percentage of Medical and Mental Health Staff Turnover, by Turnover of the Director of Jail Mental Health Services

	Same director	New director
Time with inmates		
Full-time	19%	72%
Part-time	17%	28%
Auspices		
Jail	26%	61%
Mental health agency	14%	35%
Total	17%	44%

lematic from a treatment point of view only when continuity was a concern—that is, continuity between direct care of an inmate in the jail and care of the inmate in the community. Where turnover was high, there was a decreased likelihood that staff members would be well acquainted with the external mental health system. However, since such linkages between the jail and the external system were infrequent anyway, staff turnover was not overly problematic. Furthermore, inasmuch as interventions inside the jail were usually limited to medication, continuity of care within the jail became still less important.

PROGRAM DEVELOPMENT

There were very few changes at any of the sample sites in the interorganizational linkages between the jail and other community organizations providing services to the inmates. The changes that did occur were typically beyond the control of local authorities. For example, a substance abuse agency was closed due to a lack of funding; a small firm composed mostly of psychologists was reorganized so that staff could spend more time doing research and less providing direct service; and so on. Authorities at several sites attempted major improvements, but they were almost always made within the framework of the existing service network. Accordingly, the development of jail mental health services was not as dramatic as had been anticipated, given the NIC workshop and court orders. For example, there were no changes, positive or negative, at seven sites (16%), and at only four jails (9%) were there five or more differences in the ways services were being delivered. All other jails (75%) fell into a group with only a few changes.

Small Jails

Programming at the eight small jails was especially stable. At three locations, the services were the same as they had been a year and a half earlier, both in content and in mode of service delivery. Mental health agencies did assign more staff members to work with inmates at the three sites, but most improvements, such as they were, focused on better instrument forms and procedures. New services were introduced at only two facilities; in both instances, the innovation consisted of providing in-service training for correctional staff.

Although existing services did not improve substantially, erosion in programming was minimal. The single instance of service reduction involved a decision to enhance jail security by terminating a weekly counseling session sponsored by AA. It should be noted, however, that most of the inmates at that site had been given work-release status and were allowed to attend AA in the community if they so desired.

The lack of change among the small jails seemed to have stemmed from two factors. First, the level of need was reportedly about the same as it had been at the time of our initial site visits at five of the small jail sites (63%) and had actually declined at the remaining three. The reduced need for mental health services was seen as a function of chance in one county ("Just lucky, I guess"). At the other sites, community mental health agencies, which the police had begun using in lieu of the jail, were providing alternative placements for disturbed individuals.

The second factor was financial. The mean annual budget for the small jails increased by only $1,000 (from $218,000 to

$219,000). This 0.05% increase was not even commensurate with the rise in inflation, and officials at two facilities indicated that they had lost federal grants as well. Administrators of these jails thus suffered a net loss of resources during a time when the average daily population rose from 33 to 37 (12%). Making arrangements to meet the additional costs generated by housing the extra prisoners (food, medical care, etc.) would almost certainly have to take priority over plans to expand existing services.

Medium-Sized Jails

Programming improvements at the 22 medium-sized jails were also sporadic. There were no changes at four of the sites (18%), while a new service was introduced at five jails, the most common one again being in-service training. Two innovations were particularly interesting. At one jail, officials implemented a computerized prebooking screening system to identify mentally disturbed prisoners. As a result, when it appeared that the police had brought a mentally disturbed prisoner to the jail, the director of services would be notified, and this official would then try to divert the individual to a mental health facility *prior* to admission. The other noteworthy innovation was actually implemented in response to several attempted suicides the year before. Not only were evaluation, therapy, in-service training, and case management services improved, but new inmates were also administered a special "suicide detection test" at the time of admission. No other jail in the sample used such a tool.

The most frequent change among the medium-sized jails was in the area of improved forms and procedures. Nevertheless, new medical and mental health personnel were either added to jail staffs or assigned to the jail by local mental health agencies at eight locations. One jail hired a full-time mental health/ mental retardation counselor to act as a liaison with the community mental health center following the recommendation of a special county-wide task force. The impact of such staff increases was diminished to some extent, however, by the fact that a greater number of prisoners had been assigned to jail custody. Between the time of the initial visit and the follow-up contact, the average daily population of the medium-sized jails rose from 131 to 148—a jump of 13%. Consequently, those jails that contracted for additional mental health staff time might actually have succeeded only in maintaining prior levels of service. Meanwhile, the 24 sites that did not hire additional personnel might have been in a somewhat worse position than they were at the time of our initial site visits.

A troubling development in the medium-sized facilities was that a total of 10 services were either greatly reduced or eliminated across seven jails. At three of the sites, the losses were directly attributable to budget cuts. The most serious instance of service reduction was that a mental health center could no longer respond promptly to evaluation requests from the jail, following staff layoffs at the center. Another serious situation developed when the director of a mental health center concluded that a jail's requests for evaluations frequently lacked merit and constituted an unnecessary drain on agency resources. The center thus had stopped honoring requests for inmate evaluations in nearly all but emergency cases. The final example of serious service deterioration stemmed from a decision by correctional authorities that the jail was simply not an appropriate place to treat disturbed individuals. As such, they replaced a master's-level psychologist with a social services counselor whose responsibilities included contacting outside agencies to arrange for the treatment of the most seriously ill inmates.

Unlike most officials at the small jails, administrators of the medium-sized facilities generally found that the need for mental health care had increased during the previous year and a half. At 12 sites (55%), the situation had become "more" or "much more" serious since the time of the site visit. At only 1 jail had the need declined. Illustrative of this trend may be the fact that inmates committed suicide at only 3 medium-sized jails in 1981, whereas 10 such jails experienced at least one suicide in 1982.

Community developments posed additional problems for jail administrators. Stricter laws regarding drunk drivers were cited by several respondents as a factor that would keep inmate population levels very high for the foreseeable future. State hospital closings made it more difficult for some jailers to transfer psychotic inmates, and financial cuts at mental health agencies represented an ongoing threat to the amount of staff time that could be reserved for inmates. A new assistant director at one mental health center was reportedly so unsympathetic to jail needs that she was even thought to be considering a complete elimination of jail services from her 1983 budget. The average jail budget, meanwhile, did rise by 32% (from $1,155,000 to $1,519,000) during the period under study, but the extra funds were typically appropriated for construction and salaries for new officers. Very little was left over for discretionary service development.

Large Jails

Mental health programming at the 13 large jails in the sample received considerably more attention than at either the small or the medium-sized facilities. No large sites administered the services in precisely the same manner as it had done at the time of our initial site visits. New services had been introduced in 8 jails, 1 more than the combined total initiated at the other 30 locations. In 3 of the 8 cases, staff members were instructed to develop a case management program whereby mentally ill in mates would be referred to appropriate community agencies for treatment following release from jail. Eleven of the large jails in the sample had some type of case management program in operation at the time of follow-up, although these programs were often not terribly aggressive.

It will be recalled that most of the improvement reported thus far, in the small and medium-sized jails, consisted of developing better forms and procedures. By contrast, the single most common improvement in the large jails was the commitment of extra resources to hire more staff members. Fifty-four percent of the large jails recruited more medical and mental health personnel, as compared with just 38% of the small jails and 36% of the medium-sized facilities. The average daily population rose by

12%, however, so once again it must be noted that those jails maintaining prior levels of staffing actually experienced a decline in the number of staff hours available to inmates on a per capita basis.

Individual services deteriorated at three large jails. In one instance, drug and alcohol counseling had to be cut back when the mental health center, which sponsored the program, lost funding. Service reduction at the second jail stemmed from a decision by top correctional authorities to eliminate a therapy program so that resources could be spent on other services, which were reportedly in greater demand. The most substantial deterioration, however, occurred at a site that had ironically been under a court order to improve mental health services. The problems started when the jail director hired an individual with no specific mental health training to replace a PhD-level psychologist who had been in charge of both intake screening and psychological evaluations. The situation so alarmed the psychiatrist with overall responsibility for programming that he wrote a letter to the director disclaiming any responsibility for the decisions of his new subordinate.

Respondents at 8 of the 13 large jails (62%) indicated that the problems posed by mentally ill inmates had remained about the same. At 4 locations, the problems were described as "more" or "much more" serious. An official from the sole site where problems were reportedly much *less* serious noted that a county task force had been working closely with the district attorney's office to find alternative placements for disturbed offenders. Community developments at the large jails were almost identical to those reported earlier with regard to the medium-sized facilities. The large jails, however, were more likely to have lost federal grants.

CHANGES IN SPECIFIC SERVICES

Table 6.2 presents a summary of the principal changes that occurred in the specific services studied. Only those changes for which local jail and/or mental health authorities were directly

TABLE 6.2. Program Changes in Mental Health Services

Program component				Type of change			
	Initiated	More staff	Improved/ expanded service	Procedures	Other	Discontinued/ deteriorated	Total
Screening	1	3	6	—	1	1	12
Evaluations	—	7	—	5	2	3	17
Competency	—	—	—	1	1	—	2
Psychiatric medication	—	5	—	2	2	—	9
Drug/alcohol counseling	3	3	2	2	2	7	19
Therapy	2	1	2	—	—	4	9
External hospitalization	—	—	—	1			1
Internal hospitalization	1	2	2	—	—	—	5
In-service training	5	3	6	—	1	—	15
Case management	3	1	1	2	—	—	7
Total	15	25	19	13	9	15	96

responsible are reported. Revisions in state law, for instance, could obviously have had a significant impact on jail mental health services, but might not have been the result of local initiatives. Other examples of changes that have not been included were the decision to move the forensic unit from one state hospital to another and the easing of a perceived problem for reasons unknown to those involved.

A few of the table headings require some explanation. A service has been coded as "Initiated" if it was introduced between the time of the site visit and the date of the follow-up. Conversely, if a prior service either was no longer available or had been beset by major problems, it has been noted in the "Discontinued/deteriorated" column. A site received credit for "More staff" only if the additional personnel spent a substantial amount of their daily working time providing that service. A new nurse, for example, might assist in the distribution of medication, but if he or she were hired primarily to monitor the condition of mentally ill inmates in the infirmary, only "Internal hospitalization" has been coded as receiving the extra help.

"Improved/expanded service" refers to any increase in the amount of service provided, other than that related to an increase in staff. Accordingly, some changes included very modest improvements. Officials at several jails, for example, added new questions to their screening forms in the hope of identifying more mentally ill inmates at the point of admission. Psychologists at one site supplemented their existing counseling program with special therapy for sex offenders. At another jail, eligibility requirements for case management services were eased so that more inmates could receive referrals to mental health agencies at release.

The "Procedures" column refers to changes in the process by which services were delivered. Typical examples included better communication between correction officers and mental health staff regarding the need for inmate evaluations; a nurse's placing medication in dosage packets to reduce the likelihood of error when officers distributed it; and a written agreement between jail and hospital officials that clarified the circumstances under which an inmate could be transferred to the hospital psychiatric ward.

Any remaining innovations have been coded "Other." At one site, for example, security was improved for those situations when evaluations had to be conducted at the mental health center. Dissatisfaction with the amount of time a mental health center took to respond to jail emergencies caused correctional officials at another location to contract with a separate agency for the needed services. An individual providing substance abuse counseling at a third site was replaced by someone who was supposedly much better qualified.

The table shows that the fewest developments were in the areas of "Competency" and "External hospitalization." This finding was expected because these two services were the ones over which local jail and mental health authorities had the least control. Changes in "Internal hospitalization" also appeared to be minimal, in large part because most of the jails in the sample were too small to offer this service. "Evaluations," "Drug/alcohol counseling," and "In-service training," by contrast, accounted for 54% of all changes. A total of 15 such services were introduced at the sample facilities. Officials at five sites (12%) initiated in-service training programs, the single service most commonly changed. Substance abuse counseling and case management referrals at release were the next most frequently introduced services; each was begun at three sites.

Overall, the number of initiated services was identical to the number of services that were discontinued or that deteriorated substantially. There was thus no net gain in the number of services available to mentally ill inmates. Officials at seven sites experienced problems with drug and alcohol counseling, and deterioration in this one service accounted for almost half of the overall decline. Funding cuts impinged upon the substance abuse program at three locations; officials at two sites felt that there was no longer a need for such services; and the program was eliminated at two other facilities to improve security. The therapy program suffered at four locations. In two instances, the change reflected a shift in official priorities, such that mental health personnel were assigned to do other tasks. At the other two jails, the changes were related to staff turnover: Psychologists who used to conduct the therapy sessions resigned and were either not replaced or were replaced by individuals who lacked the necessary skills. The evaluation process was the only other service that deteriorated at more than one site. One jail lost a PhD-level psychologist; a mental health center had to reduce service to another jail because of funding cuts; and administrators at a third mental health center would not honor requests for evaluations in nonemergency situations.

One-third of all recorded improvements were made in the screening and evaluation services. Common innovations in the screening program included changes in the form that was completed during booking, the assignment of professionals to conduct the screening, and the addition of a medical check or classification component to supplement the information gathered when the inmate was admitted. Much of the improvement in evaluations, by contrast, consisted of obtaining more or better-trained staff members. Other modifications focused on enhancing security and on reducing the lag time between the moment when an exam was requested and when it was actually performed.

Training was another frequently improved service, although no single strategy emerged. Officials at one jail requested assistance from the state corrections academy; two of the larger jails hired full-time training officers; and officials at two other facilities made new arrangements with local mental health agencies.

Changes in the medication-dispensing process typically entailed the hiring of extra nurses, in lieu of correction officers. At those sites where nurses were not hired, measures were initiated to reduce the number of errors that were sometimes made when nonmedical personnel were called upon to deliver prescribed drugs. One sheriff, for example, designated a special medical officer to work with the jail physician.

Drug and alcohol services were improved at nine sites. AA began working with inmates at two of the three locations where new staff members were recruited, so the jail did not always incur new expenses when making this change. Officials at one site expanded the number of weekly meetings available to inmates, but since the sessions were conducted by the same staff members who had previously been involved, there was once again no need for an additional appropriation. Group meetings were supplemented by patient education at another site, and in one jail, better-qualified personnel were recruited to replace the existing staff.

None of the remaining five services were improved at more than four sites. As previously noted, authorities have little control over the processes of competency evaluation and external hospitalization, and only a few jails in the sample were large enough to hospitalize inmates internally. Officials would, of course, have complete control over any therapy and case management programming. These services, however, were among the least frequently offered, and rarely carried as high a priority as is typically assigned to "core" services such as evaluations and in-service training.

LITIGATION AND JAIL MENTAL HEALTH PROGRAMS

One increasing approach to remedying deficits in jail mental health services has been the class action suit. This mechanism has been much more common for redress of abuses in state mental hospitals (Harvard Law Review, 1977; Leaf, 1978; Leaf & Holt, 1981) and state prisons (Brodsky, 1982). Singer (1981) points out that one of the first actions in regard to jail mental health services was a 1971 suit brought by the inmates at the Lucas County, Ohio, jail. In a sweeping decision (*Jones v. Wittenberg*, 1971), the court ruled that arrangements had to be made for inmates with "special medical problems," which has been interpreted to include mental health problems. Although this decision is over 15 years old, the number of local jails that have been sued and the volume of successful cases since 1971 is unknown. The fact that a number of jails in major metropolitan areas, such as Philadelphia, Baltimore, Washington, D.C., Chicago, Pittsburgh, and San Francisco, have had court orders to improve mental health services is apparent from media coverage. However, no systematic work has determined how many court orders have been imposed and whether inadequacies of mental health services in smaller suburban and rural jails have been the source of any successful litigation.

Not only is the volume of litigation uncertain, but its impacts are unclear. Harris and Spiller (1977) followed up three cases involving local jails plus the Arkansas state prison system, and Brodsky (1982) has reported comparative data on the responses of the Baltimore city jail and the Alabama state prison system. Both of these reports suggested that some major positive change emanated from the successful court suits. Neither, however, attempted to systematically measure the changes or the persistence of observed improvements after the order or consent decree was concluded. Furthermore, a recent General Accounting Office (1980) report contended that "while court intervention can improve conditions and is necessary in some instances, for several reasons it is not the most desirable solution for every case" (p. 10). This is so, the report argues, because broad-scale change rarely ensues, litigation is by nature reactive rather than preventive, and litigation is slow and expensive.

Because of developments in litigation, 3 of the 10 supplemental sites in our study—the jails in Clark County (Las Vegas), Nevada; Allegheny County (Pittsburgh), Pennsylvania; and Maricopa County (Phoenix), Arizona—were chosen specifically because they were under court order to develop jail programs. In addition, it turned out that 2 of the 33 jails represented at the NIC conference were also under court order—the Rock County (Janesville), Wisconsin, jail and the Jefferson County (Louisville), Kentucky, jail. In 4 of the sites, mental health services were specific issues in much broader suits. Only in Pittsburgh did the suit and court order center on mental health services alone.

During the course of our site visits, we developed a strong impression that in the absence of court orders, very little probably would have changed in the jails' mental health programs. The assistant chief administrator in one of the jails, for example, said that he hoped the court order was never rescinded because it gave him the only leverage he had in securing county appropriations. He felt that without the suit, conditions would not have improved, and that without the decree in effect, the county would back out of existing commitments. This judgment is consistent with the view articulated in a recent *New York Times* article on evolving roles for federal courts: "[M]any officials had confided to the lawyers litigating class action suits that the Federal court lawsuits and orders were the only way they could get legislatures and elected officials to provide for the policies and practices they had wanted to put into effect all along" (Rawls, 1982b, p. A-21). In another jail where mental health services had been developed over the past year, the mental health program director argued that while some change had been under way, the pending court suit had expedited program development. At a third site, the assistant director of the jail stated, "The court forced us to do certain things regarding mental health because of concern with individual inmate cases."

These and other observations suggest that the role of the courts in initiating reform in jail mental health programs may indeed be substantial. The reforms appear unquestionably to have contributed to more humane conditions. However, it is unclear precisely what types of changes have occurred; to what extent litigation or the results of litigation have actually produced the changes; and, most importantly, how much of the reform has remained or been expanded after the courts found the jails in compliance and rescinded the orders. Although our current work on jail mental health programs was not designed to answer these questions, it nevertheless strongly suggests that court intervention is important. Still, it remains unknown whether changes in jail mental health programs (made either in response to judicial intervention or of the jails' own accord) reverberate back to the broader system of community mental health service delivery. Accordingly, what is needed is a larger sample of jails than prior studies have been able to assemble, as well as more precise measurement of the changes in mental health programs following court interventions.

SUMMARY

Efforts to improve mental health programming at the sample jails during the year and a half under study met with mixed results. Services at a quarter of the jails did not change at all or actually deteriorated, either in quality or in scope. Officials at the majority of sites did succeed, however, in implementing certain improvements, but in many instances the reforms had a relatively modest impact.

The lack of sustained innovation is somewhat surprising, in view of the importance of psychiatric services and the numerous deficiencies reported at the time of the initial site visits. It could well be, however, that overcrowding has at last become so serious that it overshadows all other local correctional concerns. That is, no matter how important mental health care may be, the provision of adequate space and food necessarily assumes a higher priority.

Those sites that had made the most progress in improving mental health care were responding to a variety of forces. One site had always had a reputation for providing excellent inmate services, and the improvements were typical of what many had come to expect there. Another jail reorganized its mental health program following a rash of suicide attempts, while a special county task force was instrumental at a third location in motivating correctional, mental health, and political authorities to take the necessary action.

The role of the courts in facilitating change is not clear. Officials at two sites operating under a consent decree did, in fact, make a great deal of progress. But mental health services deteriorated at another jail, despite a court order to revitalize the program, while a court order had no apparent impact at a fourth location. Nevertheless, it is quite likely that more suits will be filed in the future. Services are not being improved at a rate that will keep pace with the rising demand, and inmate-filed suits are becoming increasingly common phenomena. In light of this, more research is clearly needed on the process of implementing court orders and on what if anything can be done to make that implementation more effective.

Chapter 7

Principles for Planning Contemporary Jail Mental Health Services

The preceding chapters have presented our major research findings concerning the organization and delivery of jail mental health services in 43 communities from various parts of the United States. We have begun in Chapter 2 with the position that current professional standards offer relatively little guidance in how to design and implement jail mental health programs. Such standards do play an important role in identifying service requirements for local jails as well as in external monitoring by the courts and statewide agencies, but they can be met in a variety of ways and currently offer little practical guidance to county or municipal officials and mental health agencies in meeting the needs of mentally ill jail inmates.

In Chapter 3, we have presented information about different approaches and practices that were followed by the 43 study jails in providing inmate mental health services. Nine basic mental health services were identified. We found that study jails ranged from ad hoc programs, which responded only to the most acute situations without any on-site service capacity, to comprehensive programs involving thorough evaluations, prompt treatment for crisis stabilization, and case management or referral to community agencies upon release.

Our major research focus, however, as presented in Chapter 4, was on the interorganizational arrangements of these programs, especially with regard to the auspices and location of the

123

jail mental health programs. Our findings indicated that no single combination of auspices (i.e., who ran the program) or location (i.e., where the actual services were delivered) was clearly more effective than any other. In one arrangement there was less conflict between agencies, but service and safety goals were not equally well met. In other service arrangements, both goals were effectively met, but interagency conflict occurred more often. In general, there was considerably less conflict between the goals of the mental health staff and the correctional staff than was expected. This was truc both for basic program goals and for day-to-day operational issues.

In the present chapter, we shift from reporting empirical findings to drawing out their implications for the development of jail mental health programs. We do this in the form of several principles or basic guidelines that local communities need to consider as part of the planning and implementation of jail mental health programs. These principles capture many of the rationale and operational features of the better jail mental health programs we encountered during the course of this study. They also incorporate our own best judgments as to how humane and responsive services can be effectively mounted for mentally ill jail inmates. We believe that these principles are generic, in that they can be applied to jails and communities of various sizes and resources.

We should point out that these principles do not constitute a "cookbook" of directives that can be mechanically applied to solve every problem of service delivery in this area. Rather, each community will have to develop the particular implementation details to fit its local circumstances. With the guiding principles discussed below, however, the basic options and strategic choices that must be considered will be more apparent, and the mechanisms for successfully achieving the ultimate goals will be more easily devised. There may be "no one best way" to organize mental health services, but some very fundamental decisions that must be made early in the planning process will influence the ultimate success or failure of any initiative in the delivery of services in this area.

These guidelines are particularly relevant for communities with an average daily jail population of 500 inmates or less. This includes all but approximately 25 of the 3,300 U.S. jails. The economy of scale of the largest facilities not only permits the implementation of options that would be impossible elsewhere, but creates a whole new series of service delivery problems—not directly studied in the research reported here—that are seldom found when relatively few disturbed prisoners are in need of treatment.

PLANNING PRINCIPLES

In order to properly address the problem of what to do with mentally ill inmates, community officials must first be sure that the issue is being considered in the proper context. All too often, primary responsibility for developing a response to disturbed criminals has been delegated to local jail officials when a much broader group of actors is actually required. The question that must ultimately be resolved is how the community, not just the jail, can best deal with the problems caused by mentally ill individuals who are arrested both for minor infractions (repeatedly in some cases) and for more serious crimes. The jail clearly has a major role to play while the mentally ill are in custody, but the development of a comprehensive, satisfactory solution to the problem requires the input and cooperation of other key actors as well. Accordingly, we arrive at Principle 1.

Principle 1. *The Mentally Disturbed Jail Inmate Must Be Viewed as a Community Issue*

In regard to mental health services, the jail cannot be considered an isolated institution. The problems addressed by these services are those of individuals who, on the average, spend very short periods of time in jail. Also, except for the "megajails" in the major metropolitan areas, it is impractical to consider developing a comprehensive set of mental health services within a jail. This is warranted neither on the basis of need nor in terms of the dollars or physical space available. It is far more practical for the jail to make effective use of community mental health centers; psychiatric units of general hospitals; private practitioners; university departments of psychology, medicine, and social work; and state mental hospitals. "Effective use" does not necessarily mean actually transferring inmates, but does mean capitalizing on the expertise of the staffs of these programs and in planning services in ways that can share program resources.

To establish appropriate services for such persons requires that the jail be seen as but one agency in a continuum of county services. Indeed, some mental disturbance is a function of the incarceration experience itself, which can be quite frightening and depressing. However, the more common mental health problems are presented by persons whose existing problems are exacerbated by jail or whose current acute episodes have precipitated their arrest and incarceration. As such, the jail is attempting to perform its custodial function of safe pretrial detention while addressing the mental health problems of a community member whose access to services is often highly restricted. Obviously, an adequate response cannot be expected if the mental health service needs are defined simply as the jail's problem. *The jail is a community institution, and the mentally disturbed inmate is a community problem.*

Thus, an important first step in responding to these issues may be to convene a meeting of the key actors from the full range of mental health agencies in the county. This includes both the public and private sectors. Clearly, many of the key actors are uninterested in or even resistant to dealing with the clientele of the jail. Nonetheless, in order to devise a strategy to address these issues, some assessment is needed of how the jail can effectively "plug into" the ongoing mental health services in the community.

To prepare for such a meeting, at least one other preliminary step should be taken—an empirical needs assessment. Since so much of what happens in interactions between the mental health and criminal justice systems is precipitated by some single heinous or tragic incident highlighted by the press, crisis responses often neglect the norm. An essential ingredient in planning for jail mental health services is a determination of exactly what the jail's needs are. Some independent clinical assessment of all residents or admissions in the jail over a period of time is of critical importance. Furthermore, it is essential to document what services were actually used in the past year or two, by whom they were delivered, and what they cost. It is not enough for the sheriff to claim that "half of my inmates are crazy and belong in mental hospitals," nor is it sufficient for the community mental health director to claim that "every inmate we have seen in the last 6 months is too dangerous to be treated in our program." A systematic assessment of actual needs in the past and projections for the future is an essential ingredient in taking this first step.

A good starting point in this endeavor is a review of institutional records to see how many inmates are referred for care every month, how many are currently receiving psychotropic medication, and so on. Surprisingly, very few jails seem to keep such records. The Virginia Beach, Virginia, city jail is a clear exception, in that officials of the mental health unit must submit detailed quarterly reports; they also maintain a special log in which the circumstances of all suicides are noted, along with comments on the known psychiatric history, if any, of the inmates involved. Elsewhere, however, not only are records seldom kept in this manner, but when they are, major discrepancies often exist in the corresponding documents maintained by mental health agencies. One small jail, for example, reported that 15 inmates were sent to the state hospital forensic unit during 1980, whereas information at the hospital indicated that there had only been 3. Administrators at another jail insisted that the mental health center had conducted a total of 390 evaluations at the jail in 1980, but the psychologist who actually performed the exams could remember only about 40. When the jail mental health chief of a medium-sized facility in the Midwest suffered a nervous breakdown, her successor was not even able to determine how many inmates were being treated or what type(s) of treatment they were being given. One jail that we had chosen as a comparison site had to be dropped from our sample altogether because no program records of any sort were maintained.

Another important component of the overall needs assessment is an examination of state and federal expectations regarding the incarceration of the mentally ill. Many states have promulgated minimum standards for the care of disturbed inmates; although such standards are often vague and/or unenforced, they nevertheless represent a potentially significant reference source. Court orders mandating the delivery of certain services will obviously have to be given close scrutiny as well, and any pending litigation alleging major deficiencies in the mental health program at the jail should pinpoint areas needing improvement even when administrators doubt the overall merit of the case.

Furthermore, it would seem useful in the context of a community-level meeting to highlight the findings presented in Chapter 5 regarding custody–therapy conflict. Contrary to some stereotypical views, correctional and mental health staffs can work together effectively. The common mental health view of inherent conflict in such settings does not seem to fit with the circumstances of the contemporary local jail. There are conflicts, of course, but usually nonessential ones. At the interorganizational level, where key actors are involved, conflicts are apt to be over dollars and who establishes criteria for admission and discharge. These latter are much more difficult to address, but with some understanding of the community nature of these problems, solutions may be forthcoming.

One example of how solutions to jail problems are linked to other components in the mental health system occurred in the Boulder County, Colorado, jail. They had encountered serious problems in finding inpatient beds in the state hospital for jail inmates for whom transfer was strongly indicated. After much pressure, the state responded by allocating a specific number of beds to each of its catchment-area counties. Boulder County was allocated 16–20 beds to which the director of the community mental health center could make direct admissions. Given the close working relationship between the Boulder community mental health center and the jail, emergency transfers are now possible, so that at any point there are usually five or six jail inmates using the Boulder County bed allocation at the state hospital.

Another important group in the community is the judiciary. Judges are frequently called upon to rule on applications to transfer mentally ill prisoners to state hospitals or to approve the involuntary commitment of someone who can no longer be cared for by his or her family. Judges must also select an appropriate disposition for disturbed individuals who have just been convicted or who have pleaded guilty to a criminal offense. The range of options includes diversion to a community treatment program, a suspended sentence whereby the person is released without supervision, probation, and confinement to a jail or prison. Finally, judges may have to render a verdict in class action suits alleging that the quality or extent of mental health care at a given jail is unconstitutional.

Although judges can thus have an enormous impact on jail operations, their jurisdiction and ability to effect lasting change is not always as strong as might first appear. It is crucial that top community officials be involved in, or at least be kept advised of, jail efforts to develop mental health programming. However, the support of political leaders may still waver unless the general public takes a broader interest in the mentally ill and provides a mandate both to improve correctional services and to explore noncustodial ways of responding to disturbed offenders.

Jail administrators cannot expect to obtain increased funding for mental health services if neither the public nor the county executive understands the gravity of the situation. For example, a special task force established to study the mental health program at the Salt Lake County, Utah, jail recognized this fact and recommended that a broadly based citizens' advisory council be formed to work with the mental health center and jail project coordinator. The task force also recommended that community education efforts be increased through the use of newspapers, television, radio, and personal contacts, so that local citizens would become more aware of problems stemming from the incarceration of mentally disordered inmates. The chief administrator of another jail held a news conference to highlight the need for better care, and gave newspaper photographers a tour of the

facility's aging infirmary and isolation cells. His comments resulted in a series of newspaper articles and editorials that ultimately helped to persuade the county commissioners to appropriate funds for a major renovation. In short, a jail cannot be
expected to adequately address the mental health needs of its
inmates if it is seen as an isolated institution. A productive set of
first steps to counteract this perception could be the aforementioned needs assessment and community-level meeting.

Principle 2. *The Jail Is and Should Remain
Primarily a Correctional Facility*

Local adult correctional facilities in the 20th century are designed for the purpose of incarcerating criminal offenders.
Padded cells, observation tiers, and other devices that may be
used in managing the mentally ill are intended only to help
jailers meet the most pressing physical and psychological needs
of men and women who cannot be freed to seek professional
attention elsewhere. A jail is not meant to be used as a specialized type of mental institution.

Given the importance of caring for disturbed inmates and
the frequent inability of officials to transfer such individuals to
state hospitals, the temptation may nevertheless exist to expand
the level of mental health care at the jail to a point where all but
the most psychotic prisoners can be handled internally. Although this may seem advantageous in the short run, there is a
serious danger that any such concentration of services will ultimately cause both the police and judges to view the jail as an
appropriate place to send mentally ill persons who do not really
have to be incarcerated. A physician serving on the Allegheny
County (Pittsburgh), Pennsylvania, prison board explicitly
warned jail authorities about this likelihood:

> Those of us who have been in private practice have all seen the
> kind of person you just can't handle due to the extent of their
> mental illness. If you have a place for them, these people will be
> sent to the jail without committing any crime. I foresee this hap-

> pening—imaginary offenses to get these people in there—and
> we've got to make sure that unless a person commits a criminal
> offense he just can't go there. ("Thirty Six Percent of Guards Not
> Trained," 1980, p. A-16)

A similar concern was voiced by members of a task force studying proposals to establish a separate mental health unit at the
Milwaukee County, Wisconsin, House of Correction. The head
of the county's protective services management team stated em-
phatically, "We don't want to make it better to treat mentally ill
people through the criminal justice system than through the
mental health system because that's a crime against the people
being treated" ("Isolation Cells for Mentally Ill Criticized,"
1980, p. 5). Such an arrangement would also make the task of
managing the jail more difficult and increase the risk that other
prisoners will assault or be assaulted by someone who does not
have full control over his or her actions.

Ironically, the practice of sending the mentally ill to jail so
that they can take advantage of the services available there can
ultimately contribute to a vicious circle of sorts, whereby the jail
will need even more resources in the future to treat the increased
number of disturbed inmates in custody. If more staff members
are then hired to accommodate the greater demand for professional care, correctional officials will simply reinforce the community image of the jail as a resource center for the mentally ill
who are caught breaking the law. Administrators thus need to
protect the welfare of those who must be confined, but if the sole
or primary reason for confinement is their need for mental
health services, they should not be in local jails.

Principle 3. *Serious Mental Health Needs among
Inmates Require Limited but High-Quality
Professional Services in Every Jail*

Although no one would argue that the county jail is an ideal
location for delivering either medical or psychological treatment, there are clear needs that must be met. Federal courts have

consistently ruled since 1899 that correctional officials must provide at least basic medical care (Carrabba, 1981). Moreover, the U.S. Supreme Court has held that failure to provide adequate treatment constitutes a violation of the Eighth Amendment when it results from "deliberate indifference to a prisoner's serious injury or illness" (*Estelle v. Gamble*, 1976, p. 105).

The leading judicial opinion pertaining to the delivery of mental health services in jail was issued in response to a lawsuit filed on behalf of prisoners at the Allegheny County, Pennsylvania, jail. In *Inmates v. Pierce* (1980), a U.S. circuit court of appeals concluded that although most challenges to prison medical care had focused on the alleged deficiencies of treatment for physical ailments, there is no reason why the adequacy of mental health care should not be held to the same standard. In reaching that decision, the court cited *Bowring v. Goodwin* (1978), in which another circuit court of appeals had stated flatly that there is "no underlying distinction between the right to medical care for physical ills and its psychological or psychiatric counterpart." The court of appeals concluded that the "deliberate indifference" standard of *Estelle v. Gamble* is applicable when evaluating the constitutional adequacy of mental health care provided at a jail or prison. The key factor in determining whether a system for providing psychological or psychiatric care is constitutionally adequate is whether inmates with *serious* mental or emotional illnesses or disturbances are provided "reasonable access" to medical personnel qualified to diagnose and treat such illnesses or disturbances.

After ruling that jail inmates are, in fact, entitled to receive mental health care, the court remanded *Pierce* to the U.S. district court for western Pennsylvania to consider the specific remedies that would have to be implemented in order to bring the Allegheny County jail into compliance with the requirements of the U.S. Constitution. Inasmuch as this facility (average daily population of 440) is among the largest jails in the country, many of the changes that the court ordered would probably not be expected of jails that are considerably smaller. The underlying principle that guided the court in selecting those changes, however, is probably equally valid for all local adult correctional institutions:

> The jail is not a mental health facility, nor do administrators intend that it become one. It must, however, be staffed and organized to meet emergency situations, to make appropriate referrals, and to carefully care for and protect those who must be housed in the jail for whatever reasons despite their mental illness. (*Inmates v. Pierce*, 1980, p. 643)

The issue of staffing is particularly important. The court ruled that whenever the ratio of professional staff to inmates having serious mental health problems constitutes an effective denial of access to diagnosis and treatment by qualified health care professionals, the "deliberate indifference" standard is violated. The exercise of informed professional judgment regarding the serious medical problems of individual inmates under such circumstances is precluded by the patently inadequate size of the staff. One of the first things that the superintendent of the Allegheny County jail thus had to do to satisfy the terms of the court order was to hire more trained personnel to tend to inmate needs.

It should be pointed out that the limited availability of community resources is no defense against charges of inadequate inmate care. A federal court has stated explicitly that "lack of funds is not an acceptable excuse for unconstitutional conditions of incarceration" (*Finney v. Arkansas Board of Corrections*, 1974, p. 201), and this argument was rejected in the aforementioned Allegheny County case as well. As long as a county chooses to operate a jail, it must provide specialized care for the health needs of its inmates, regardless of taxpayer opposition or other seemingly mitigating circumstances.

The necessity to provide minimal services does not diminish the fact that the diversion of disturbed offenders, who do not pose a serious threat to the public safety, may still be a major objective for more appropriate service delivery. The National Advisory Commission on Criminal Justice Standards and Goals

(1975), the National Coalition for Jail Reform (undated), and the Advisory Committee on Intergovernmental Relations (1983) have all taken the position that jails are not designed, equipped, or staffed to handle the mentally ill and that incarcerating the mentally ill is inherently unfair in any case. They also note that many communities have had a great deal of success in diverting minor offenders to agencies or institutions that *are* equipped to handle the disturbed.

Most efforts of this sort focus on diverting the mentally ill before they are actually taken into custody. In some instances, responsibility for diversion has been assigned directly to specially trained police officers. In Galveston County, Texas, for example, several sheriff's deputies have been certified as "emergency medical technicians" and have received special training in crisis intervention and casework principles at the regional mental health center. The deputies are available around the clock to work with mentally ill people encountered by law enforcement personnel (National Coalition for Jail Reform, undated).

Other police agencies have chosen to work with mental health professionals who can respond to crisis situations as they occur. Perhaps the best-known model of this type is that developed by Montgomery County Mental Health/Mental Retardation Services (MCRS) in Norristown, Pennsylvania, which was cited as an "exemplary program" by the Law Enforcement Assistance Act. MCRS is a private, nonprofit corporation founded in 1974 to meet the immediate, short-term needs of psychiatric and drug/alcohol emergencies on a 24-hour basis. It has a total staff of 138 employees and operates a fully accredited psychiatric hospital with 33 beds. When local law enforcement officers encounter a disturbed person, they can call MCRS to request an ambulance with trained mental health counselors, who then treat the person at the scene or provide transportation to a hospital or other appropriate facility (Blew & Cirel, 1978). Between February 1974 and December 1982, more than 35% of all MCRS contacts were criminal justice referrals. A 3-month study of 152 police referrals indicated that charges were finally brought in only 34 cases (22%). The total annual cost for all

MCRS services after third-party payments was approximately $250,000.

A comparable program, somewhat more limited in scope, is based in Fairfax County, Virginia. In 1977, the county community services board established a mobile crisis unit to meet emergency mental health needs between the hours of 4:00 P.M. and midnight. The unit provides the police with immediate, on-the-scene assistance for a variety of calls, including domestic disturbances, suicide threats, substance abuse problems, and episodes of acute psychiatric disturbance. In 1979, unit personnel were able to implement a nondetention resolution in 421 (73%) of the 581 cases in which a field visit was made. A controlled outcome study completed in 1979 found that the mobile crisis unit reduced the percentage of involuntary detentions by 47% over the number of detentions that could have been expected to occur without the unit's intervention. A follow-up study of patients who were not detained revealed that 71% had followed through with referrals and were actively engaged in a voluntary treatment program 4 weeks after the intervention (Fairfax County, VA, 1981).

Police officers in counties that do not have mobile crisis teams often have no choice but to arrest a suspected mentally ill person who is creating a disturbance. Diversion efforts at these locations must then take place prior to sentencing, often while the individual is in custody. The locus of such a program may be the district attorney's office, a court clinic, or the public defender's office. The Boulder, Colorado, community corrections department has a pretrial services unit with a special bond coordination/supervision program, wherein mentally ill prisoners are interviewed and referred for treatment in the community when appropriate.

Programs such as those described above offer humane, cost-effective alternatives to incarceration. Many communities do not have the resources to develop similar services, however, and informants at several of the sites we studied indicated that the local district attorney would be reluctant to divert known offenders in any case. Even mental health officials occasionally questioned the desirability of diverting the mentally ill, on the grounds that mental illness alone rarely excuses the commission of illegal behavior. So, although diversion can be both effective and appropriate, it does not have universal support. In any case, it does not represent a total solution to the current jail mental health crisis, since even jails in communities with strong diversion programs already in place still report ongoing problems with disturbed inmates who cannot be diverted. Thus, under any circumstances, some core mental health services are necessary for the jail inmate population.

Figure 7.1, depicting the mental health services offered at the detention facility in Contra Costa, California (average daily population of 244), schematically presents an actual model of the type of program we are recommending. The reader will note that efforts to identify the mentally ill go far beyond the simple administration of a screening instrument at intake. Mental health staff members accept referrals from a variety of sources and have the capacity to respond promptly to emergency situations. Once the mentally ill have been identified, those who are acutely disturbed are referred to inpatient psychiatric hospitals. Others may be given outpatient care in administrative segregation or in the general population, depending upon the extent of perceived dangerousness. Ancillary facilities, such as a "rubber room" and an observation room for suicidal inmates, are also available for use as the need arises. The hallmarks of this system are promptness and flexibility, and it places a premium on inmate management rather than on treatment in the classical sense. Prisoners who are still in need of professional care when they are released are encouraged to accept a community placement appropriate for their particular needs.

Principle 4. *Correctional Administrators Should Concentrate on Developing Mental Health Services in the Areas of Identification, Crisis Intervention, and Case Management at Release*

The research reported in this volume did not set out to analyze the substantive aspects of jail mental health programming.

Rather, our focus was on investigating the organizational and interorganizational aspects of service delivery. Nevertheless, it became apparent during our conversations with correctional and mental health staffs involved in jail mental health programs that many practitioners had similar views on the appropriate function and relative importance of the various services.

The types of mental health services that are most basic for the local jail become apparent from the fact, discussed in Chapter 5, that jails are "people-processing" institutions (Hasenfeld, 1972). That is, jails are short-term facilities whose primary function is to provide inmates with a disposition (or more appropriately, to keep them until the court classifies them) for some other organization to handle (e.g., a state prison, county probation, or a pretrial diversion program). Their focus is not on long-term detention and basic personality change or rehabilitation. When the jail is seen for what it is, the mental health services that need to be emphasized become clear.

Accordingly, the three principal mental health needs in planning jail services are identification, crisis intervention, and case management at release. This package de-emphasizes broader treatment objectives, and, as such, it contrasts with what the jail administrators in our study tended to highlight in their program descriptions. Almost inevitably, when asked about the mental health program at a jail, the sheriff or chief administrative officer would describe the number of hours per week the psychiatrist was in the jail; the number of nurses available to monitor medications; a special housing tier for mentally disturbed inmates that facilitated their treatment; and so on. In short, what they tended to discuss was their *treatment* program. Rarely did we spontaneously hear of a thorough screening program; of mental health practices that could be rapidly deployed for stabilizing volatile, mentally disturbed inmates; or of linkages with community mental health services upon release.

In contrast to those services centering on treatment, the programs we surveyed that appeared to provide the most humane services while most effectively aiding the jail operation were those that de-emphasized traditional treatment in favor of early identification, appropriate short-term interventions (in the

FIGURE 7.1 Contra Costa Detention Facility Mental Health Services

1. Request from deputy in booking or intake module

   Mental health staff to booking or intake
   Evaluate inmate and determine level of service required

   Acutely Mentally Disordered
   (in danger to themselves or others or gravely disabled)

   Refer to inpatient psychiatric hospital

   If no beds available, refer to medical/psychiatric module

   Community Placement
   Inpatient psychiatric facilities

   Residential halfway houses

   Board and care homes

   Outpatient clinics
   Vocational services
   Monthly follow-up

2. Early identification of mental disorder through screening within 72 hours

   Mental health clinical staff interviews anyone expected to stay at least one week

   Mentally Disordered-Unstable
   Medical/psychiatric unit
   • 24 hour care
   • observation room for suicide risk
   • rubber room
   • 20-25 beds in single rooms

3. Referrals from:
   - Court
   - Deputy
   - Self
   - Medical or substance abuse staff

Immediate response or appointment scheduled at earliest convenience

Mentally Disordered and Extremely Dangerous
Administrative segregation
Outpatient services provided by clinical staff

Mentally Disordered-Stable
General housing - outpatient services

Not Mentally Disordered, But in Crisis
General housing - volunteer or staff to provide crisis counseling

Prison Referral
For continuity of care

form of either psychotropic medications or specialized housing units), and effective collaboration with community resources to maintain the persons in the community after their release so that they were not quickly rearrested. The mental health personnel at one such program observed that treatment in their jail really meant two things: (1) "helping people deal with the reality of their incarceration"; and (2) "getting the inmates in touch with themselves to be able to recognize their problems and agree to seek care upon release."

Clearly, such program priorities do not supplant the need for professional psychiatric attention to individual inmates. Unless mentally disturbed, acting-out inmates are identified early, they may do serious injury to staff and other inmates or to themselves. However, for such inmates or for less seriously disturbed inmates, psychiatric treatment in the classical sense of individual or group therapy sessions is not feasible, given the jail's functions. The prescription of medication and recommendations for special housing tiers, when the latter are available, constitute the limits of appropriate treatment in such cases.

Just as identification may be seen as an ingredient of the treatment program, so too can case management. Teaching short-term inmates where to go for help may frequently be more important than treating them in the jail. Two of the facilities in our study addressed this problem by having mental health staff split time between the jail and community agencies. In Contra Costa, California, a psychiatric resident rotates through both the jail and the community mental health center during her weekly duties. Inmates can thus be seen by the same service provider while in custody and after their release. Prisoners are considered more likely to follow through on their appointments if they know in advance whom they will be dealing with and have already had an opportunity to develop a working relationship. Likewise, some of the mental health personnel in the Boulder County, Colorado, jail are actually on the community mental health center's payroll and are assigned for a specified number of hours per week to the jail primarily for screening and case management.

Case management need not, of course, be limited to the making of appointments with specific mental health professionals. If an inmate is on psychotropic medication, the jail psychiatrist may want to call a pharmacy to insure that there is no lapse in the prescription. In Contra Costa, California, the jail provides transportation to a halfway house if this is deemed appropriate by the medical or social service staff. Job placement services can also be very helpful, since two-thirds of the mentally ill offenders identified in one study were unemployed at the time of their arrest (Arthur Bolton Associates, 1976).

A case management service can be structured in several ways. Some jails refer all mentally ill prisoners in need of continued care to community agencies. Facilities with more limited staffing resources may have to limit referrals to a particular subgroup of the mentally ill, such as those on medication or those who are involved in a therapy program. It should also be pointed out that while mental health professionals should obviously have a great deal of input in deciding the specific nature of the referral, the person who coordinates the program can be a corrections officer or member of the social services staff. This flexibility is desirable because boundary-spanning activities require more organizational and communication skills than actual clinical experience. One of the coordinator's most important tasks, for example, is to assess existing community resources in order to determine the agencies' service eligibility requirements and overall organizational goals.

One method of addressing this concern and simultaneously enhancing the continuity of care is to have the mental health center staff member who is called in to evaluate an inmate at the jail make an appointment to see the inmate after he or she has been released. Such an arrangement is already in place at the Gwinnett County (Lawrenceville), Georgia, jail, and seems to be working well. Another way of providing the service in order to give mental health primary responsibility has been implemented at the Salt Lake County, Utah, jail, where the mental health center has assigned employees to work full-time at the jail. The counselors not only make appointments for inmates to receive further care from appropriate community agencies upon release, but they give the inmates the telephone number of the jail mental health unit and encourage them to call back in the event that they have any difficulties obtaining the recommended care.

Jail officials may be frustrated in their efforts to develop a good case management program by the lack of community resources capable of providing aftercare services. The U.S. Department of Justice specifically raised this issue in its defense against criticism from the General Accounting Office concerning the way in which inmates were released from federal detention centers (Rooney, 1980). Also, in a recent review of 129 mental health halfway houses, only 9 expressed a willingness to serve offenders (Goldmeier, Sauer, & White, 1977), while in rural areas a lack of resources is reported to be particularly acute (Harding and & McPheeters, 1979; Kirk & Spears, 1979).

If the jail concentrates on developing these core services of identification, crisis stabilization, and case management, and makes no pretense about its intent or ability to treat the mentally ill, judges may be less inclined to send disturbed individuals to jail for the sole purpose of receiving specialized care. In the absence of community alternatives, the police may still use local correctional facilities to detain mentally ill offenders who do not need to be incarcerated. Jail services should not, of course, be developed to a point where money that is best allocated to community mental health centers is actually being spent at the jail. One of the correctional officers with whom we spoke even mentioned somewhat wryly that if the NIC really wanted to improve the jail's position *vis-à-vis* the mentally ill offender, it should use its influence to lobby for better mental health center funding. Jail services should be designed to help inmates cope with the stresses of incarceration, while efforts to address the broader goal of long-term treatment are best reserved for other agencies in the community.

Principle 5. *There is No One Best Way to Organize a Jail Mental Health Program*

Jails can accomplish the objective of protecting inmates' mental health in a variety of ways. In fact, an approach that is both desirable and feasible at one location may be totally inappropriate somewhere else. Different strategies are needed because county jails vary so greatly in size, structural characteristics, level of perceived need, and resources available in the community's existing mental health service network. Even jails that house a comparable number of disturbed inmates and are architecturally similar may have widely disparate funding bases and different types of mental health agencies in the community that are willing to serve jail clients. The director of the community mental health center at one site, for example, absolutely refused to provide professional assistance for inmates. He argued that since most inmates' needs existed long before the individuals were arrested and none ever bothered to seek treatment while they were free to do so, they had no right to expect special attention now that they were in custody.

Given that a jail is seeking to distribute its available resources to emphasize identification, crisis stabilization, and case management, there is no single arrangement that can provide all of these services optimally. Whether to establish a contract with a local group medical practice for all mental health services, to enter into a shared staffing arrangement with the local community mental health center, or to hire full- and/or part-time staff on the jail payroll is a decision that depends upon a whole host of historical, political, fiscal, and community factors. These decisions also depend upon the relative amount of conflict or number of coordination problems with which the jail administration is willing to deal. As we have noted in Chapter 4, certain linkages tend to produce more conflict and coordination problems between jails and mental health agencies, whereas others decrease effective service delivery but reduce conflict.

In many ways, the solution to the problem of how best to arrange services should emerge for each jail from the successful conduct of the actions listed above in connection with Principle 1. The process of, first, identifying those persons in the community who should be included in a discussion of mental health services and, second, analyzing programming issues, should provide the basis for identifying the optimal service structures for a jail.

Some sample sites did this very well. Most prominent may have been the sheriff of Whitman County, Washington, who even managed to win a seat on the mental health center's board of directors to insure that the jail's needs would be taken into account when the board met to establish annual priorities. Jail officials at most locations, however, make plans for program services in a much more informal manner and suffer somewhat predictable results. A task force assembled at one large Eastern city commented, "The county mental health/mental retardation system is unclear as to what its role should be with regard to the jail. Most base service units who have clients at the jail are uncertain what their responsibilities are." A report on service delivery at a large Western jail similarly noted that "There is no written statement of responsibility for the mentally ill inmate. Verbal agreements between the sheriff and public mental health have been both confusing and misleading as to which agency has follow-through responsibility." The research committee of the task force on mentally ill criminal offenders at a third site found that "The population at issue has not been defined, the magnitude of the need is unknown, and the needs are essentially unassessed. Service providers and officials at neither the jail nor the county mental health system understand the workings or limitations of either system." The bottom line is that there must be appropriate linkages between the jail and existing providers of mental health services in the community. Just what form these linkages take depends on both the wide range of resources available and the goals of the county for the jail mental health program.

A REGIONAL MENTAL HEALTH APPROACH?

Jails in rural counties tend to be especially hard-pressed in finding ways to manage the mentally ill. The local tax base is usually very limited, and there are sometimes no area hospitals or mental health agencies willing and able to help. One possible solution may be the formation of a mobile mental health team that visits several rural jails on a regular and as-needed basis to evaluate prisoners and provide whatever treatment is possible. Some jails in our study were already doing this with apparent success.

Another way of assisting these facilities may be to designate a regional jail for disturbed inmates who cannot be managed elsewhere. The jail would have an observation unit, padded cells, and an infirmary. Staffing would be provided by specially trained corrections officers and psychiatric nurses. Treatment services would still be limited primarily to crisis intervention, so that the jail would not be confused with a mental hospital, but at least the inmates would be housed in a secure, nonthreatening environment.

Three types of inmates could ideally be transferred to such a jail. The first would be that group of mentally ill prisoners who can no longer be safely managed at the jail where they were initially housed. A second group would consist of inmates who have just been discharged from a mental hospital and who must now be returned to the custody of a sheriff. Correctional administrators complain that these inmates often deteriorate in custody, so that the regional jail could serve as a kind of halfway house until it is determined that the inmates are fully stabilized. Finally, the jail should be able to accommodate any disturbed female prisoner who is being held in the catchment area. Even some of the larger urban jails in our sample were often unable to address women's needs in the same way that men's needs were met, because of unavoidable structural limitations (the infirmary could not be partitioned to serve both sexes, the observation tier was located in the men's wing, etc.).

Precedent for a regional jail can be found in some sheriffs' practice of sending all females and/or juvenile prisoners to another county where the jail has separate facilities for them. The New York State Office of Mental Health operates a facility on the grounds of the Central New York Psychiatric Center for jail inmates from 16 counties with acute mental health needs. Each jail provides its own transportation and pays a prorated fee for security expenses to Oneida County, where the center is located.

The successful operation of a regional jail that handles mentally ill prisoners would obviously be predicated on the development of very clear lines of clinical and administrative authority. The criteria for transfer would also have to be understood and accepted by all concerned, so that the jail would not become a depository for all disruptive inmates. Other problems such as those stemming from a possible change of venue would have to be worked out. Responsibility for administering the mental health unit could be assigned to at least three different actors. Many respondents in our sample, for example, felt that the mental health system should take the initiative. Others argued that local law enforcement agencies are now being given a higher priority than county mental health centers, so that any arrangement of this sort would be more likely to receive funding under the guise of corrections. Still others pointed out that intercounty cooperation has historically been extremely poor and that no sheriff would agree to have such a unit in his or her jail in any case. The Lancaster County, Pennsylvania, forensic services task force therefore recommended that the state establish a regional forensic psychiatric facility similar to the one in New York. Consistent with the "no one best way" concept, officials in each locale will have to review the advantages and limitations of each approach and decide which seems to make the most sense for them. Nonetheless, the concept of a regional jail for mentally ill inmates from rural counties of modest size is a concept that warrants close examination.

IMPLICATIONS FOR PRACTICE
AND RESEARCH

The research we have presented in this volume was geared toward producing some basic organizing principles for developing jail mental health services. Our goal was to be able to offer some fundamental guidelines that could be put into practice. In many ways, the five major principles we have discussed in this chapter are probably less concrete and directly implementable than jail administrators would like. However, a research foray such as this should not be expected to deliver some specific directives. The widely differing types of jails and unique sets of community problems and relationships require the application of general principles to specific circumstances. Although such an approach does not offer exact steps toward developing jail mental health services, the guidelines presented, if followed in the general order discussed here, can provide excellent strategic guidance to anyone (jail administrators, county executives, or community advocates) wishing to systematically improve what are often horrendously inadequate services.

In fact, the primary use of these principles may be to alert the planners or initiators of new mental health services to the strategic decisions that must be made. Rather than focusing on questions such as what type of or how many staff members are needed, whether it is more cost effective to contract for services, or where the budget items should be placed, we have become sensitized to what appear to be the overriding questions and assumptions that must be addressed at the outset and from which the specific practices would flow.

It should also be apparent that a core ingredient to developing appropriate services is better information. The planning process requires detailed data on the level of need in the jail, as indicated by prior use of services and current clinical assessment. It requires a comprehensive mapping of the mental health services in the community, how they fit together (if they do), how they are financed, and how they are linked to the social welfare and educational systems (especially higher education and professional schools). In short, the jail cannot develop mental health services in a vacuum. There are complex sets of working relationships even in the smallest counties. Unless some initial reconnoitering is done, the most effective and least costly approaches may be overlooked. Research at the outset of service development or overhaul is critical, as is some periodic feedback about how the service arrangements are working. This type of information is essential to good jail operation and may be imperative if any litigation occurs.

In the end, it should be kept in mind that although we have mentioned many positive features of the 43 jails we visited, the level of care at the sample jails was often inadequate in both scope and quality. This finding is particularly alarming, in light of the fact that mental health services at these facilities are in all likelihood much better than what would be found in a random sample of U.S. jails. As noted in Chapter 1, 33 of the sites were represented at training workshops where participants learned a variety of skills pertaining to the planning and implementation of mental health services. The supplemental sites were selected on the basis of either their reputation for offering exceptional inmate services or the introduction of a variety of reforms as a result of judicial intervention. As such, all of the communities visited had demonstrated an interest in inmate mental health needs that probably far exceeds the norm. Moreover, most American jails are much smaller than those included in the sample, and small facilities tend to be the least able to provide services of any kind. There is thus every reason to believe that the quality of mental health care in our nation's jails is as problematic today as it was 15 years ago, when concerns were first expressed about the welfare of deinstitutionalized mental patients who might wind up behind bars. Our hope is that the guidelines that have emerged from this research may help communities to address these acutely serious problems more effectively.

III

FROM PRINCIPLES
TO PRACTICE

The New York State Local Forensic Suicide Prevention/Crisis Intervention Program

A major difficulty often encountered in converting general planning principles in any field into action is the absence of concrete examples of relevant applications. We hope to mitigate that problem in this volume by providing a detailed account in this chapter of a recent application of the principles developed in this volume. (Chapters 9 and 10 describe two additional examples of programs exemplifying the principles.) The application involved the development of a suicide prevention/crisis intervention program in seven New York county jails by the New York State Office of Mental Health and Ulster County Mental Health Services in collaboration with some of our research project staff. This initiative is reflective of the five central planning principles articulated in Chapter 7. Through learning how one component of a jail mental health program was so constructed, readers should be better able to apply the five general planning principles to any program components they may wish to develop. For analysts or students of organizations, the chapter may more concretely depict how an interorganizational perspective can contribute to actual program development.

The reader should know, however, that members of the program staff within the Office of Mental Health Bureau of Forensic Services initially conceived of the program without benefit of these planning principles. Quite probably, had our research staff not become involved in the planning process, a workable service delivery model would have been created and implemented. However, as detailed below, when we began collaborating, we did help develop a service model and procedures consonant with the planning principles. Thus, the program originated in the expertise of the Bureau of Forensic Services program staff, but its final structure and processes were developed in concert with the results of the research reported in the preceding chapters.

The particular project that was developed around these planning principles focused on the delivery of crisis intervention services to inmates in rural and urban county jails and lockups throughout New York State. The New York City jails were excluded, because of their unusually large size and because administrators of those jails have fairly ready access to local hospital beds for inmates who are acutely mentally ill. The overriding strategy of the crisis program was to train the staffs of a small number of jails and police lockups to systematically screen all incoming inmates for suicide potential and then to refer high-risk inmates to mental health personnel, inside or outside the jail, in order to assure timely and appropriate interventions. Similarly, emphasis was placed on assuring that the mental health professionals were responsive to the jails' requests. This program initiative marked an unusual collaboration between multiple segments of state government on the one hand and local correctional, law enforcement, mental health, and political communities on the other.

PROJECT BACKGROUND

In New York State, there are a total of 178 police lockups and 57 jails outside of New York City. These 235 facilities hold about 7,500 inmates on any given day. These facilities are widely dispersed throughout a 57-county area that covers approximately 50,000 square miles. The lockups, which are used to detain arrested persons for up to 48 hours pending arraignment, are administered by town, village, and city police departments. The local sheriff, an elected county official, is responsible for operating the jail in all but 1 of the 57 counties.

Suicide is the leading cause of death among prisoners in jails and lockups in New York State, as well as in the United States as a whole (New York State Commission of Correction, 1985; Charle, 1981). The suicide rate for prisoners being held in these facilities is 3½ times higher than that of the general population, and it is 5 times higher than that reported for inmates in state correctional institutions (Danto, 1973). Although not all suicidal persons are mentally ill, the evidence suggests that over half of all locally incarcerated prisoners who killed themselves in 1983 had a record of prior inpatient psychiatric care (New York State Commission of Correction, 1985). Commission investigators maintain that at least some of these suicides might have been averted if the prisoners had received timely mental health services.

Another factor that makes the phenomenon of inmate suicide so alarming is that the number of suicides and suicide attempts in jails and lockups has been increasing steadily in recent years. In New York State, the number of successful suicides in jails and lockups outside of New York City increased from 17 in 1983 to 24 in 1984, an increase of just over 41%. The number of suicide attempts requiring hospitalization during the same 1-year time period rose by 15%, from 196 to 226 (New York State Commission of Correction, 1985). The trend toward more successful suicide attempts can be attributed in part to the fact that there has been an increase in the absolute number of prisoners in custody.

A second and perhaps equally important reason for the observed increase in jail suicides is that many police departments are enforcing drunk-driving laws more systematically than has been the case in the past. The Massachusetts Special Commission to Investigate Suicides in Municipal Detention Centers (1984) found a direct correlation between tougher drinking driver measures and the incidence of lockup suicide attempts. The commission pointed out that as many as 70% of recent lockup suicides and attempts had occurred among persons charged with driving while intoxicated or other alcohol-related charges. Ninety percent of those suicides were committed within 4 hours of admission to confinement, while the individuals were either still drunk or in the process of becoming sober. New York, like Massachusetts, has enacted strict laws prohibiting driving while under the influence of alcohol. Lockups in New York are thus similarly likely to experience a relatively high number of suicide attempts because of the rising number of individuals who are being arrested for this offense.

A third impediment to effective suicide prevention/crisis intervention services is the fact that many of the jails and lockups in New York State have been unable to overcome serious administrative barriers that impede effective service delivery and that were found in our study to exist throughout the country. Interorganizational linkages tend to be weak; identification procedures are often inadequate; and crisis intervention care is only available at selected sites and times. Some local facilities in New York have outstanding mental health programs, but others are clearly struggling and have been doing so for several years.

The New York State Commission of Correction, which oversees operations of all adult correctional facilities in the state, provides technical assistance to jails and lockups for the purpose of enhancing the safety and welfare of all persons being held in custody there. The New York State Office of Mental Health Bureau of Forensic Services likewise offers its expertise to such facilities and has limited funds available for a variety of local assistance projects. Although both agencies have made progress pursuing common goals at individual locations, it had become apparent by 1983 that a united, system-wide approach would have far greater potential impact than merely continuing their efforts to help individual counties. The first initiative to emerge from these renewed relationships was a joint suicide prevention crisis service project. Funding for the project came from NIMH (Mental Health Services Manpower Systems Development Program Grant No. STC-63T23MH15378-0751) and the New York State Office of Mental Health.

We became involved in developing the suicide prevention/ crisis intervention program at the point when the Bureau of Forensic Services was drafting a request for proposals that would be sent to the directors of all community mental health centers in the state. As originally conceived, the grant recipient would have been responsible for developing both a service delivery model—a package of crisis intervention procedures for jails and lockups—and a variety of training materials that could be used to help implement the procedures. The basic approach being proposed was for materials to be developed that could be supplied to any participating county, so that its own jail and lockup staffs could be trained in proper identification and response procedures for inmates in serious mental distress.

Following discussions between our project staff and the staff of the Bureau of Forensic Services, it was decided that an optimum approach would be to divide the original work plan into two components. The first component would include both the design of the service delivery model and an evaluation of the program. The second segment would include the developing of the training materials and the actual implementation of the model in three to five counties. In this way the ideas developed in the research project described in the earlier chapters, which represented the major data in this area, could be brought to bear directly on a problem of immediate and substantial import.

It was thus decided to assign primary responsibility for overall program development to the Office of Mental Health Bureau of Survey and Evaluation Research. For the other component, a request for proposals was distributed statewide to find an interested mental health center that was qualified to develop the training materials and cooperate in the development of the model. A second request for proposals was distributed for the purpose of identifying counties interested in demonstrating the model once the procedures and training materials had been prepared.

The Bureau of Survey and Evaluation Research contract called for the timely completion of four principal activities. First, a literature search was to be conducted to identify existing crisis service models for jails and lockups, the roles that officers played in them, and ways of facilitating coordination of joint mental health–criminal justice agency endeavors. Once the literature search was completed, the second task would be to create a realistic crisis intervention service model. The third task specified in the contract was to collaborate with the outside contractors in their development of an intake screening instrument and training program. This collaboration would assure that they were consistent with the goals and objectives of the model. Finally, the bureau was directed to design a methodology that could be used to evaluate the benefits and limitations of the crisis model. (This last activity is not relevant to the issues here, so it is not discussed further.)

The agency that was awarded the training contract was Ulster County Mental Health Services. Ulster County assembled an interdisciplinary team consisting of clinicians, administrators, and media experts to work on the grant. It is important to note that although the Bureau of Survey and Evaluation Research was responsible for writing the first draft of the model's procedures and Ulster County was primarily concerned with training needs, there was close collaboration between the groups. Procedures drafted in the Bureau of Survey and Evaluation Research, for example, were routinely distributed for feedback to Bureau of Forensic Services staff, Ulster County staff, and the members of an advisory committee that will be described later. Their comments were used as the basis for the subsequent revisions of the model. Only through such a dialectic could we move from planning to specific operational procedures.

The training program developed by Ulster County Mental Health Services was approximately 8 hours in length. The training had six principal modules: the role of the correction officer in preventing suicides; background information about suicide in general; substance abuse; mental illness; the suicide prevention screening guidelines; and site-specific documentation and referral procedures.

As part of the training, correctional personnel were to view an original 40-minute film in which professional actors portrayed inmates and officers in a variety of thought-provoking situations. The film was designed to be stopped at several points for classroom discussion. Facility officials were to be given a detailed manual outlining how the course should be taught, and all participants would receive a special 20-page handbook summarizing key points of the training. The model's procedures dictated that shift commanders receive an additional 8 hours of mental health training each year, but specific arrangements for this instruction would have to be made through local mental health agencies.

THE INTENT AND STRUCTURE
OF THE PROGRAM

Our research from the 43 study sites made it clear that although a model for jail crisis intervention services must have considerable flexibility, several substantive elements must be present in any jail mental health program. Figure 8.1 presents a schematic overview of the New York State program and includes all of the components that we consider to be critical. In the next two sections, we describe the key elements of the specific model developed for this program, and then describe how the model was implemented in two counties with very different demographic characteristics. Most of the program description presented here outlines the way in which the model would be implemented in a jail setting. Several components would also be applicable to police lockups, but would require some scaling down because of the more limited resources and the different nature of a lockup.

In accordance with Principles 3 ("Serious mental health needs among inmates require limited but high quality professional services in every jail") and 4 ("Correctional administrators should concentrate on developing mental health services in the areas of identification, crisis intervention, and case management at release"), the model for the jail suicide prevention/crisis intervention program places a very heavy emphasis on the identification and timely referral of suicidal and mentally ill inmates. Procedures were specifically drafted on the premise that timely identification can only be accomplished through an ongoing process and that this process should continue for the entire time that a prisoner is in custody, not solely at intake.

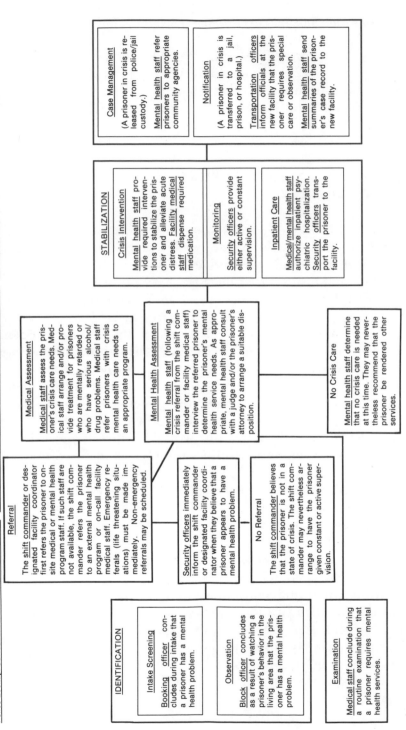

FIGURE 8.1. The New York State forensic suicide prevention/crisis service program (New York State Commission on Corrections, 1986).

Identification

The identification component of the model was designed to assure that correction officers would be particularly sensitive to a prisoner's state of mind during intake. According to a national study conducted by the National Center on Institutions and Alternatives (1981), over 50% of all jail and lockup inmates who committed suicide during 1979 did so within 24 hours of incarceration, and another 20% killed themselves during the first 14 days. These findings are consistent with those of Danto (1973), Beigel and Russell (1973), and others, who have similarly reported that inmates commit suicide more frequently during the initial weeks of custody than at any other time of their incarceration. Authorities estimate, moreover, that 8 out of 10 people who kill themselves give prior verbal or behavioral warnings of their intentions (Farberow & Shneidman, 1965). Given proper training and procedural guidelines, officers should thus be able to identify a substantial proportion of all inmates who are seriously thinking about harming themselves.

Transporting Police Officer

The model procedures direct jail personnel to draw on several sources of information during intake to identify individuals who may be at risk. The booking officer must first ask the transporting police officer whether a new prisoner has displayed any unusual behavior or made statements suggesting that he or she is suicidal. All too often, police officers drop prisoners off at the jail without pausing to share information that would be of great interest to the correctional officials who are responsible for providing an appropriate level of supervision. It is anticipated that problems stemming from this lack of communication can henceforth be avoided.

Suicide Prevention Screening Guideline Form

Booking officers then complete a Suicide Prevention Screening Guideline Form for each prisoner prior to placing him or her in a cell. The form has a total of 15 items printed on a 1-page document, which then becomes part of the prisoner's permanent record. The items are divided into three categories. The first, personal data, consists primarily of yes–no questions posed directly to the inmate. The questions explore such areas as psychiatric history, prior suicide attempts, and the nature of current relationships with significant others. In the second part of the form, the booking officer is told to record a series of observations about the prisoner's behavior and appearance. Key indicators include signs of depression, unusual anxiety, and intoxication. The final section of the form addresses the individual's criminal history. Research suggests that prisoners who are most likely to commit suicide are those who have been arrested for the first time and those who have been arrested on four or more occasions (Ulster County Mental Health Services, 1984).

This form was developed through reviewing the extant literature and conducting a 1-month pilot test. The pilot test was conducted at one medium-sized jail (average daily population = 119) and one small police lockup. During the month in which the form was being tested, all 119 prisoners admitted to the jail and all 30 prisoners detained at the lockup were screened as a routine part of the intake process. We collected the forms and conducted interviews with booking officers that focused on such areas as question clarity, prisoners' willingness to discuss personal matters, and the effect of the screening on the officers' other responsibilities. Shift commanders were questioned about the ways in which the screening process affected overall operations. Results generally confirmed the value and practicality of the suggested guidelines, but produced several minor modifications of the form.

In the final version, prisoners deemed to be at risk on any of three specified questions are automatically referred to the shift commander, who must decide whether additional action (e.g., increased supervision and/or referral to mental health professionals) is warranted. Other prisoners who receive a total of seven or more checkmarks in the high-risk column likewise are automatically referred to the shift commander. Also, booking officers are encouraged to inform their commander about any prisoner whom they personally believe to be suicidal or in need of special mental health care, regardless of the results of the screening instrument.

Central Rolodex File

A third strategy to facilitate the identification of prisoners need-ing special care at intake involves the use of a central Rolodex file containing the names of all inmates who have either at-tempted suicide or required inpatient psychiatric treatment while in custody. It is recommended that the file be arranged alphabetically and updated as needed. By checking these records as part of the routine booking process, an officer can readily determine whether a given prisoner has needed extraordinary mental health care during a prior incarceration at the facility. Increased supervision may be both appropriate and necessary for such a prisoner, even though the individual exhibits no outward signs of crisis during the 5 or 10 minutes that are needed to complete the booking process.

Friends and Relatives

A prisoner may, of course, become suicidal or develop serious emotional problems several weeks after being admitted to jail. Sentencing is frequently a traumatic experience, a spouse may file for divorce; and the unrelenting pressure of living in an uncertain situation that one is powerless to change may simply overwhelm an individual's ability to cope satisfactorily. The model thus contains several strategies to be used apart from the initial screening, to increase the likelihood that indicators of pending crisis displayed subsequent to booking will be recog-nized and reported in a timely manner.

One of these strategies is to solicit the assistance of the prisoners' friends and relatives. Even the most observant officers may not be able to recognize changes in a prisoner's tempera-ment as readily as those who have lived or grown up with the inmate, and it is much more likely that a prisoner will confide suicidal thoughts to a long-standing friend than to an officer. Another key feature of the model, therefore, is the requirement that a sign be posted in visiting areas requesting that visitors inform jail officials whenever a prisoner seems unusually de-pressed or is experiencing personal difficulties of a traumatic nature (e.g., divorce or death of a parent).

Tier Log and File Card

Relevant information about third parties is recorded in the tier log, along with any observations that a block officer may make regarding a prisoner's emotional state. Procedures require that officers review this log at the beginning of each shift so that they will be familiar with any developments that have occurred since their last tour of duty. Many jails already mandate this routine review, but interviews conducted with correction officers while the model was in the developmental stages indicated that valuable insights can be lost when a prisoner is transferred to another part of the jail. Officers supervising inmates on the new tier may learn, for example, that a certain individual was recently the subject of a one-on-one suicide watch, but have no idea as to what upset the inmate or what they should look for in the future. To eliminate this problem, the model includes a procedure requiring officers to record critical data on a 4″ × 6″ pink file card, which then accompanies the prisoner during any future housing assignments.

Mental Health Assessment

Only professional mental health personnel have the qualifications to assess the magnitude of a suspected crisis, of course, and to determine whether clinical intervention is actually warranted. The procedures built into the model thus require a close working relationship between jail and mental health personnel. In this fashion, mental health staff can be called upon, on both an emergency and a nonemergency basis, to assess prisoners whom the officers believe to be at risk. Prisoners who appear suicidal or seriously mentally ill and in immediate danger of inflicting serious self-injury are classified as requiring emergency assessments. Prisoners who are incapacitated by drugs or alcohol to the degree that they pose a threat to themselves, others, or property also fall into this category. Another requirement is that emergency assessments be available to jail staff 24 hours a day. The model also notes that emergency assessments should be completed within a time that assures the safety of the prisoner and is considered reasonable by the sheriff and community service director. If, during the assessment, it becomes apparent that the prisoner requires psychiatric inpatient care, the examining clinician is directed to arrange for the prisoner's prompt admission to an appropriate hospital (or, if the clinician does not have the authority to do this, to arrange for the prisoner to be immediately evaluated by staff members having such authority).

Nonemergency assessments are rendered to determine a prisoner's immediate need for crisis stabilization and prevention services. They are usually scheduled in advance and conducted on site within the correctional facility. Nonemergency assessments are provided for prisoners who are chronically mentally ill or who behave in a manner that suggests they are experiencing acute emotional distress. The assessments must be completed within a time period that is consistent with the degree of urgency indicated by the referral.

Referral and Intervention

It should be noted that assessments are only to be provided when it appears that an inmate needs immediate services to assure his or her continued safety and welfare within the facility. It is not recommended that evaluations be provided for individuals suspected of having personality disorders, minor neuroses, or other nonthreatening mental conditions. This is consistent with our Principle 2 ("The jail is and should remain primarily a correctional facility"), which warns against making the treatment of marginally disturbed inmates an expected feature of daily jail operations. This philosophy is also embodied in the procedures specifying the intended goals of proposed treatment services: stabilizing acutely mentally ill prisoners, maintaining seriously mentally ill prisoners at an appropriate level of functioning during their incarceration, and arranging psychiatric inpatient services for mentally ill prisoners when necessary. The focus here is clearly on providing crisis intervention services only. There is no pretense about trying to "cure" a client or resolve long-standing personal conflicts.

Principle 4 ("Correctional administrators should concentrate on developing mental health services in the areas of identification, crisis intervention, and case management at release") is similarly specific in its emphasis on crisis intervention rather than long-term verbal and behavioral therapies. In addition, the principle calls for case management at release, and case management is an important part of the crisis model. No one, of course, can be forced to seek outpatient care under normal circumstances. Those inmates who do wish to be referred to appropriate service providers, however, should be assisted by mental health personnel and/or jail medical staff. Linkages are to be made where appropriate with substance abuse and mental retardation agencies, as well as with various mental health programs.

Some inmates who leave the jail in a state of acute crisis will be destined for state prison rather than home. Case management referrals to community service providers are obviously pointless in these situations, but the model is clear in specifying that both jail and mental health authorities have certain responsibilities in facilitating the continuity of care at the receiving institution. Specifically, the shift commander at the jail must be sure that officials of the new facility are immediately informed of any signs of suicide potential or serious mental health problems exhibited by the prisoners, and/or of any psychotropic medications that have been prescribed for them. Mental health professionals are directed to prepare and forward treatment summaries to the clinical personnel responsible for services at the prison.

Underlying all of the model's policies and procedures is a fundamental concern with the quality of both direct and indirect services provided as part of the crisis program. This is consistent with Principle 3, which specifies that jail mental health programming should be structured so as to meet high professional standards ("Serious mental health needs among inmates require limited but high-quality professional services in every jail"). In the absence of new funding for more staff or facility renovations, the best way of working toward this goal may be to require more training for personnel and to draft procedures that increase the individual and organizational accountability of all concerned.

The model's procedures demand increased individual and organizational accountability by formalizing the annual planning process, strengthening communications, and increasing the amount of documentation describing actions taken on behalf of mentally ill inmates. Two full pages in the procedures manual outline the role that local government units[1] are asked to play in the planning and development of jail mental health services. There was some confusion in the past regarding how the responsibilities of these units applied to county correctional institutions, so the new procedures are very clear in defining what is expected. Included in these expectations are developing and monitoring of service agreements between local mental health programs and the jail; making efforts to assure the timely availability of emergency and nonemergency assessments at the jail; and convening a meeting at least annually with the sheriff to review the state of jail mental health services. The sheriff, in turn, is directed to collaborate with the jail medical staff in collecting statistics and other relevant data needed to determine current service needs. This information can then be used when the sheriff meets with authorities of the local government unit to correct any deficiencies that may exist in the service delivery process

The model's procedures enhance the quality and frequency of communications in several ways. Medical personnel, for example, are directed to cooperate with mental health authorities in the development of inmate treatment plans and to advise correction officers of any side effects that they should watch for when a prisoner is taking psychotropic medications. Mental health personnel are instructed to consult with correction officers at least once a day regarding the condition of any prisoner who receives increased supervision for mental-health-related reasons and to take the time to explain to the officers why a

1. In New York State, the "local government unit" is a unit of the local government authorized by the city or county to plan for and provide publicly funded mental health services.

particular disposition is most appropriate for a given inmate. Mental health staff members are also supposed to be given an orientation to the jail, so that they will not inadvertently violate facility rules and regulations. Correction officers, meanwhile, are ordered to advise the jail medical staff immediately when an inmate refuses to take psychotropic medication, and to consult with the mental health staff regarding the proper management of inmates known to be suicidal.

Most of the documentation requirements outlined in the model were drafted with the correction officer in mind, since most medical and mental health personnel already make suitable entries in a client's file whenever services are provided. Officers are directed to maintain a written record of all instructions, significant observations, and actions taken pertaining to mentally ill or suicidal inmates. Service referrals, first aid procedures, and insights provided by family members are all illustrative of the types of information that must be documented. In imposing these new obligations, the drafters of the model made a conscious effort to keep reporting requirements to a minimum; some documentation is critical, however, to assure that important information is passed on to the next shift and to assure that officers carry out their responsibilities. Log entries can also serve to protect the officers in any lawsuit alleging inadequate care, if it can be shown that they have done everything expected of them in the prescribed manner.

Our Principle 5 asserts, "There is no one best way to organize a jail mental health program." The crisis model has been designed so that it can be implemented at jails of all sizes. As such, it favors a service model relying on external service providers. This pattern is particularly common in New York State, where even the largest jails rarely employ their own mental health personnel. It is nevertheless clearly stated that the model can be implemented in a variety of ways. In fact, jail administrators wishing to implement the suicide prevention/crisis intervention model were given a special workbook designed explicitly to help them adapt the policy and procedures manual to their site-specific needs. Some of the procedures have even been drafted in a way that calls attention to the variety of service delivery arrangements that can be used to implement them. Thus, while the New York State local forensic model has similar substantive programmatic features for every jail, the ways in which it can be implemented may vary according to what makes the most sense locally.

PROGRAM IMPLEMENTATION

The actual implementation of the crisis service model requires extensive multiagency planning and cooperation of the type described in Chapter 7 in our discussion of Principle 1. There is a widespread consensus that the incidence of suicide and mental illness among jail inmates is a serious problem that warrants immediate attention; however, the task of transforming this concern into an actual program necessitates the active involvement of several important groups. Thus, community input was actively sought when the program procedures were in draft stage.

Two agencies that were particularly important in the early conceptual stages of this project were the New York State Commission of Correction and Ulster County Mental Health Services. The Commission of Correction has the authority to establish and enforce program standards at jails throughout the state, and it joined forces at an early date with the state Office of Mental Health as a cosponsor of the crisis project. As previously mentioned, Ulster County Mental Health Services was the agency selected to develop the training materials to teach correction officers about suicide and crisis intervention generally. Ulster County staff also worked closely with the Office of Mental Health and the Commission of Correction in refining the model's procedures.

Looking toward the eventual implementation of the crisis program, the planners gave priority to the goal of forming a knowledgeable and influential advisory committee at the early stages of the development of the model. As we have noted in

Chapter 7 in our discussion of Principle 1, "The jail clearly has a major role to play while the mentally ill are in custody, but the development of a comprehensive, satisfactory solution to the problem requires the input and cooperation of other key actors as well." It thus made sense to form a committee to assure that the procedures were realistic; to see that they were consistent with the goals and mandates of the agencies that would be called upon to provide services; and to review early drafts of the model with an eye toward suggesting changes that would streamline or otherwise improve the model as a whole. Involving the advisory committee in this manner improved both the quality and credibility of the final product. It also served to create a sense of ownership among key organizations that would later prove valuable during the demonstration phase of the program. Calling the project a "local forensic program" rather than a "New York State Office of Mental Health program" kept a host of potentially serious "turf" issues from arising, and the task of obtaining the cooperation of key agencies and service providers during implementation became much less problematic.

Six of the eight organizations that agreed to serve on the Advisory Committee were directly affiliated with New York State. The day-to-day task of caring for locally incarcerated prisoners obviously rests with the individual jurisdictions that maintain the jails, but it was generally acknowledged that the state has an important role to play in helping these localities address the problems posed by inmates who are mentally ill and/or suicidal. Introductory comments in the policy and procedures manual note that "State agencies have specific responsibilities, defined by agency mandates, relevant to the tasks of reducing the risk of suicide in jails, developing mental health services for underserved mentally ill persons, and training correctional officer staff" (New York State Commission of Corrections & New York State Office of Mental Health, 1986, p. 4). State agencies participating on the advisory committee included the Division of Alcoholism and Alcohol Abuse, the Division of Substance Abuse Services, the Office of Mental Retardation and Developmental Disabilities, the Division of Criminal Justice

Services, and two bureaus within the Office of Mental Health (Children and Youth, and Education and Training). Representatives of the Governor's Task Force on Alcohol and Criminal Justice also served on the committee, along with representatives of two professional groups, the New York State Sheriffs' Association and the New York State Association of Chiefs of Police. The Committee was thus broadly based and had the power needed to pursue a united, system-wide approach to the development of jail mental health services in New York State.

All procedures, the training curriculum, and other project materials needed to implement the model were developed between March 1 and December 31, 1984. Six counties containing 7 jails and 28 lockups were then chosen to participate in a 1-year demonstration and evaluation of the model, beginning on April 1, 1985. The participants in the demonstration ranged from the two largest non-New York City counties in the state (with average daily jail populations of approximately 400 and 1,000 inmates, respectively) to a county with one of the smallest jails in the state (with rarely more than 40 inmates in custody).

Since the demonstration project has just entered the implementation phase as this chapter is being written, it is too early to speculate on the ultimate impact of this initiative. However, a great deal of information has already been collected on the way in which officials of each county set out to implement the model. By sharing some of their experiences, we hope that we can illustrate how our planning principles have been applied in real-world settings. To illustrate the flexibility of the model's application, the discussion that follows focuses on the two counties that are the largest and the smallest of those involved in the demonstration. The discussion demonstrates that while the planning principles were drafted primarily with the small and medium-sized jails in mind, correctional officials can successfully apply them in large metropolitan settings as well. Contrasting the experiences of an urban and rural site also serves to highlight the ways in which the planning principles can be used in very different situations.

Implementation of the Model at an Urban Jail

The largest county participating in the demonstration covers a densely populated area near New York City. The county jail has an official maximum capacity of 938 inmates, but in recent years has housed somewhat more than 1,000 prisoners on any given day. Even then, the sheriff routinely sends prisoners to other county correctional facilities because the jail is simply too small to meet local needs. Medical services are provided by three part-time physicians who work a total of 60 hours at the jail, four registered nurses, and eight emergency medical technicians. The jail has an infirmary for inmates requiring close medical attention, but none of the available beds are used for the mentally ill.

Outpatient mental health care is provided by the county department of mental health, mental retardation, and developmental disabilities. The county medical center has a secure five-bed psychiatric unit for prisoners and provides emergency detoxification services as well. Male inmates who are suicidal and/or mentally ill can be placed on one of two tiers. The tiers can accommodate 48 inmates with double bunking, but 63 inmates are usually assigned there. A half tier containing eight cells is reserved for the mentally ill women.

Preliminary data suggested that mental health services at the jail were not adequate, given the level of need. The mental health observation tiers were overcrowded, and there were many other inmates whom the officers would have assigned there if more room were available. In 1983 alone, the jail reported 1 successful suicide and 39 serious suicide attempts and, at that time, there were three different lawsuits related to suicide and other mental health care issues pending against the facility.

Overall responsibility for implementing the crisis model at this site was given to the county department of mental health, mental retardation, and developmental disabilities. Senior officials of this agency, the jail, the county medical center, and the county department of drug and alcohol addiction all provided input in the planning process and had final authority regarding the role that their respective agencies would play in the program. Authority for the day-to-day planning and oversight, however, was given to a project director employed by the county mental health agency. The person selected to serve in this role was an accredited and certified social worker who had been serving as the assistant director of forensic services for the county. His duties included supervising the operation of the jail's mental health clinic, so he was already very familiar with correctional procedures and had a close working relationship with on-line and administrative personnel at the jail.

The project director participated in a variety of important activities. First, he served on a local ad hoc advisory committee that was formed to oversee the overall development of the crisis program. He also worked closely with jail officials to help draft mutually acceptable policies and procedures, and he played a major role in training corrections staff members involved in the identification and referral of suicidal inmates. In addition, the director was expected periodically to evaluate the use of the intake screening guidelines by jail officers, in order to make sure that the guidelines were administered in a consistent manner. Among his other responsibilities were to monitor the implementation of the program very closely and to act as the principal liaison officer with appropriate agencies to resolve any disputes that happened to arise. This last function was considered especially important, since it is almost inevitable that problems will arise during the initial stages of any new program initiative in which several agencies are called upon to upgrade and coordinate services. Finally, the director had to make sure that quarterly reports and all data needed for the evaluation were submitted in a timely manner.

The jail's representative in the development of the crisis project was the facility's chief training officer. This individual had worked at the jail since 1973 and had served as a desk officer, floor supervisor, and deputy tour commander. He helped to draft the procedures, scheduled officers for training, and presented several of the lectures included in the training program.

Most of the counties involved in the demonstration received a one-time grant of $25,000 to help offset the costs of implementing the crisis model. The project director of this county used the funds to hire a full-time jail social worker to help assess inmates referred for care by correction officers. The person chosen for this position had been working evenings at the jail during the preceding year. The officers respected him, and he knew jail procedures very well. The grant was not, however, sufficient to reimburse the county for the time invested by the project director, nor did it offset administrative costs such as those for typing and filing. More significantly, the grant did not provide the money needed to pay for the overtime expenses that would be incurred while training the jail's 442 line officers and 28 shift commanders.

Inasmuch as the sheriff was committed to full implementation of the program, money needed for training was taken from funds that had been set aside for other overtime expenses. The project director and jail training officer conducted the training in several stages between April and December of 1985. The first class was reserved for tour commanders and other high-ranking staff members. The second class targeted booking staff, transportation officers, and medical personnel. These sessions were completed prior to implementation and cost approximately $20,000. Subsequent training sessions were to be offered for the remaining officers, who were usually assigned to watch prisoners in the cell blocks. The overtime expenditure needed to run these sessions would also be very high, but it would be a one-time expense, in that future instruction on the program model for all new officers would be included in the basic orientation that recruits receive prior to their first assignment.

The projected expense of implementing the crisis model as a whole was a source of concern to mental health personnel as well as jail officials. Inmates appearing to need emergency psychiatric care during the night had formerly been taken to the county medical center for assessment, and shift commanders indicated during training that they would be much more likely to make such referrals once the new identification procedures went into effect. In fact, the volume of referrals made to mental health personnel would probably increase during all three shifts because lack of space made it impossible simply to transfer suicidal inmates to the observation tier. The sheriff would have liked to open a new observation tier, but the cost of having just one officer at this site supervising suicidal prisoners exclusively on a 24-hour basis 365 days a year would be approximately $150,000.

Despite the agreed-upon importance of the suicide prevention/crisis intervention program, neither the jail nor the jail's mental health service providers had extra staff members who could be reassigned from other tasks in the event of a substantial increase in the number of prisoners believed to be suicidal. Ultimately, extra funding might have to be appropriated to fully resolve the anticipated problems. In the meantime, however, new procedures were adopted that appeared to have satisfactorily addressed many of the more troublesome issues. There were no current plans to open a new observation tier, for example, but the sheriff did direct that inmates with serious mental health problems should never be placed in isolation and that they should be given "appropriate" supervision. Medical staff were to play a more active role in evaluating suicidal prisoners, and staff members at the medical center met with the project director to discuss ways of reducing the amount of time that prisoners would be held at the emergency room pending emergency psychiatric examinations. The project director reported, "Things are going very well as we approach the start of the project."

Implementation of the Model at a Rural Jail

Program planning at the smallest county in the demonstration involved similar agencies, but a very different set of problems. This jail is in a very isolated rural location and derives most of its revenue from tourists who ski in the winter and camp during the summer. The jail has an average daily population of 40 inmates. Inasmuch as the jail has a capacity of 48, the sheriff frequently accepts prisoners from other jurisdictions.

The jail has no infirmary, is not accredited, and relies on a part-time doctor and hospital emergency room for medical services. Mental health care is provided by the small county mental health department, which has a shared staffing arrangement with a state psychiatric center. Traditionally, the mental health department has sent a staff member to the jail on an as-needed basis. All inmates admitted to the facility are automatically placed in a special six-cell observation tier, where they receive constant supervision for the first 48 hours of their incarceration. They are then transferred to another part of the jail, where they are checked every 15 minutes unless their behavior indicates that they should remain on observation. The observation tier is rarely full. The one point of similarity between this jail and the urban jail described in the preceding section is the urgent need for improved mental health care services. In 1983, this rural jail reported 1 suicide and 12 serious suicide attempts. The sheriff has been sued twice since 1980 for reasons related to inmate suicides and mental health care.

The county responded to the Office of Mental Health's request for proposals to demonstrate the model in cooperation with a larger adjacent county. No funds were awarded for implementation to the county being described, but officials of the mental health department of the adjacent county did receive $25,000 and agreed to provide ongoing technical assistance to their neighboring counterparts.

Most of the planning done prior to implementation was handled by the jail warden and an accredited certified social worker from the county mental health department, who was the project director for forensic mental health services. The social worker also served as the project director for the crisis program, and as such was assigned a variety of responsibilities similar to those given the project director in the first county described.

Since the jail was not awarded any money to offset start-up costs, one of the first priorities was to obtain extra funding from the county legislature. The warden and project director submitted a joint proposal that led to the hiring of a new forensic mental health worker with an MSW degree. The person hired was assigned to work half-time at the jail and half-time with the family court. Local judges had wanted a mental health staff member assigned full-time to the family court and resisted efforts to have him serve the jail as well, but the warden and project director were able to lobby successfully for the dual responsibilities.

The next issue that had to be addressed was that of training correctional staff. The jail has 17 full-time officers, 5 part-time officers, and 4 shift commanders. Nearly all of the officers were trained in a single 8-hour session conducted by the project director and the forensic mental health worker. Officers' response to the training was very positive. Unlike the staff of the first county described, where the officers were overworked and felt somewhat upset about their new responsibilities, the officers here tended to be more enthusiastic, and many stayed after class on their own time to continue discussing the program. One officer confided that her father had committed suicide and that the training had greatly helped her to understand his motivation. The sheriff was so enthusiastic about the training that he ordered officers to put their names on the pre- and posttests completed for the evaluation. These tests were administered in an anonymous fashion elsewhere, but the sheriff wanted to identify those who did not receive passing grades. These officers were instructed to study the suicide training handbook and then take the test again when they felt that they could pass. The sheriff was also considering giving the training to his road deputies.

Early reports from the rural county indicated that the crisis program was going very well. The smaller scale of operations there meant that fewer agencies participated in the planning process and that logistical problems were easier to resolve, but the required preparation still represented a substantial investment of limited staff time. A thorough needs assessment was required, and procedures had to be drafted that would address serious inmate mental health needs with very limited agency resources. Long-standing local disputes pertaining to how quickly mental health staff responded to requests by jail staff and the way in which state inpatient commitment laws should be used also had to be resolved. Planning for jail crisis services is thus a challenging endeavor in both small and large communities. It appears, however, that the planning principles can be applied equally well in both settings.

Early feedback has been extremely encouraging, but we are still unable to say whether or not implementation of the crisis model will enable jail officials to achieve the goals for which the model was designed. It does, however, appear that the planning principles constitute a valid, constructive basis for developing jail mental health services. Substantively, the model incorporates all of the elements recommended in Principles 2 through 5. A broadly based advisory committee consisting of professionals with a variety of backgrounds and disciplines participated in developing the model from its earliest conceptual stages. At no time were any suggestions offered that would implicitly or explicitly violate the program parameters recommended by the planning principles.

The utility of the community planning process outlined in Principle 1 was demonstrated twice—first at the state level, when the advisory committee came together to draft the model procedures, and then again at the demonstration sites, where police, correctional staffs, mental health personnel, and substance abuse officials met to share information and determine the optimal way of pooling resources to provide crisis services locally. The program could not have been implemented successfully without the cooperation and input of all these key players.

The central thrust of the planning principles is that the jail should only be used to house prisoners in accordance with established functions as defined by legal and historical mandates, and that jail programs having ramifications for the public as a whole should only be planned with active community involvement. Although the specific focus of the planning principles is on inmate mental health services, the relevance of the principles is not limited to this single area. Jail overcrowding, sentencing guidelines, and alternatives to incarceration are all examples of serious public safety issues affected in one way or another by the role that the jail is given in a particular locale. There should be a clear understanding of what the jail can and cannot do, and county legislators should seek widespread community input before proceeding to make fundamental systemic reforms.

In conclusion, we should point out that attempts to apply the planning principles in any context should be preceded by a thorough site-specific needs assessment. Those who develop programs without adequate data inevitably run the risk of seeing their efforts fail as a result of faulty assumptions and erroneous perceptions. The notorious case is a poor basis on which to redesign a system. We have demonstrated that with sufficient preparation, jail and mental health administrators in New York State have been able to successfully develop a crisis intervention program that is consistent with our planning principles. We are optimistic that administrators in other states can apply our planning principles to resolve other specific problems as well.

Chapter 9 ────────────────────────────

The Palm Beach County, Florida, Forensic Mental Health Services Program: A Comprehensive Community-Based System

Joel A. Dvoskin

The Palm Beach County, Florida, Forensic Mental Health Services Program is designed to be a fully comprehensive, county-based service system for all persons receiving mental health services while involved in the criminal justice system and for those on conditional-release statuses after inpatient care is completed. This program was developed through the lead of a community mental health center, closely collaborating with a public defender's office and a county jail. It was developed during the mid-1980s, quite independently of any of the planning principles that have been articulated in Chapter 7. Nevertheless, its conceptualization and implementation demonstrate how these planning principles can work to produce a truly exemplary program.

The description of this program consists of a component-by-component critique adapted from a consultant's report to the program's operators as to how they could further improve the program's functioning in early 1986. When the description is

Joel A. Dvoskin. New York State Office of Mental Health, Albany, New York.

explicitly linked to the planning principles, as is done in the latter portion of this chapter, this approach provides insights that may facilitate the application of these key principles in a wide variety of other forensic settings, not simply in local jails.

BACKGROUND

In May 1986, the 45th Street Mental Health Center in West Palm Beach, Florida, requested an outside evaluation of the Palm Beach County Forensic Mental Health Services Program, for which the center was the chief administrative unit. The general goal of this program was drawn from *Guidelines for Community Forensic Mental Health Programs,* a document developed by the Florida Department of Health and Rehabilitative Services' Office of State Mental Health Programs. Drawn up in August 1984, these guidelines proposed:

> Within each district services for clients involved with the Criminal Justice System should be as comprehensive as those provided to other clients. It will require, however, certain services unique to their circumstances and must in some cases be delivered where the clients are incarcerated. (Florida Department of Health and Rehabilitative Services, 1984, p. 1)

The general orientation of these guidelines, as well as the specific program components described therein, are consistent with the principles articulated throughout this book. The guidelines call for the following:

1. Screening.
2. Pretrial evaluation.
3. Posttrial, presentence investigation.
4. Evaluation that will provide information for probation determination and process.
5. Treatment services (i.e., outpatient services in jail or elsewhere, inpatient services in a receiving facility, day treatment, and residential services).

6. Case management services aimed at linking all of these service elements to a consumer and at coordinating the system to achieve a successful outcome.

During a site visit in May 1986, three things quickly became clear. First, despite years of experience in observing, evaluating, and managing various correctional and criminal justice mental health programs, neither consultant (myself and Dr. Steadman) had ever observed a program that had attempted to address the needs of the community, the client, and the criminal justice and mental health systems so comprehensively as the one in Palm Beach County. Second, it was obvious that this program had made a direct and successful effort at following the Florida Department of Health and Rehabilitative Services guidelines described above. On the negative side, however, there was deep-seated disagreement at that time regarding the political, legal, clinical, and, indeed, moral role of the program. One major disputant in this disagreement appeared to be the public defender's office, which regarded the clients' legal interests as the primary focus of the program, and therefore regarded itself as the appropriate lead agency. The other major disputant was the 45th Street Mental Health Center in West Palm Beach, which managed the program.

OVERVIEW OF PROGRAM

In order to understand the Forensic Mental Health Services Program, it is essential to recognize how mental health services may come into play at the various stages of the criminal justice process. Figure 9.1 depicts these stages, the services provided by the Forensic Mental Health Services Program at each stage, and the various staffs from both the criminal justice and mental health systems who are involved at each stage.

As Figure 9.1 makes clear, it is impossible to adequately evaluate a full community forensic system simply by looking at any one of its service elements (e.g., evaluation) in any one facility (e.g., the jail) rather than its full array of services and

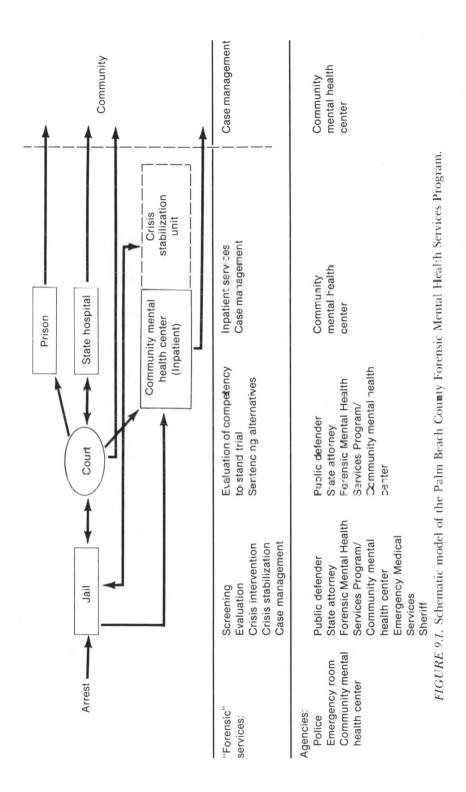

FIGURE 9.1. Schematic model of the Palm Beach County Forensic Mental Health Services Program.

facilities. In reviewing this program, I follow the sequence (from left to right) in Figure 9.1. Before assessing the specific program elements, however, it is first necessary to discuss some generic issues of the program's administration.

Program Administration

Program Management

There was a tendency for the people interviewed on site to understand only the specific program components within which they functioned. Although there were notable exceptions, who had an appreciation of the comprehensiveness and inter-connectedness of the entire program, it was more common for service problems to be defined rather idiosyncratically. This failure is especially troubling, since a particularly valuable aspect of the program is its comprehensive and integrated nature.

Figure 9.1 graphically demonstrates that the program's service responsibilities encompass both the jail and the community, plus a number of state institutions (e.g., prisons, civil and forensic state hospitals). Therefore, the locus of management control for the program seems most appropriately to reside with the community mental health center staff, whose normal responsibilities cover all of the settings and services in which forensic mental health clients may find themselves.

In assessing the most appropriate alternative for management of the Palm Beach County program, we considered all of the agencies that had an interest in it. The county criminal justice system, including both the sheriff and the jail administration, were viewed as inappropriate, since their responsibilities end at the point at which the accused is delivered for trial or at the completion of a misdemeanor sentence. It does not extend into other dispositions, such as release into the community.

Similarly, the public defender and the state attorney's office see their responsibilities ending at the point at which the criminal charges are disposed of and all appeals exhausted. The state Department of Health and Rehabilitative Services, while appropriately involved in the planning of services, is not a direct provider of services for people at the county level; this is the responsibility of county agencies of one type or another. It was therefore concluded that the responsibility for the overall management of this program should be with one or more community mental health centers.

The community mental health center has responsibilities for individuals at every stage depicted in Figure 9.1. Since the jail is a community institution, the center should be responsible for individuals who are in the jail, and particularly for linking people in the jail with community services. The community mental health center also should be responsible for citizens who are at large in the community following court disposition (e.g., through conditions of probation). Other program clients include individuals who have satisfied the claims of the criminal justice system and are at large in the community, but in need of specific services and case management. Inmates in the jail who need inpatient services can be appropriately served by a crisis stabilization unit, which was in the process of being developed in Palm Beach County at the time of our visit. Furthermore, when individuals who have been found incompetent to stand trial or not guilty by reason of insanity are returned to the community, there is no other actor involved in the program who has any legal responsibilities for these individuals until they commit another offense. Again, only a community mental health center has legal and conceptual services responsibilities for these individuals at every stage of the process.

Written Policies and Procedures

Given the numerous program components and the large number of individuals who are processed weekly in each of these components, it is absolutely essential that at every stage of service provision there be written policies and procedures. Such policies and procedures can serve a number of important purposes:

1. They define exactly the persons who are responsible for each service at every stage of the process, what exactly

they are responsible for doing, and the time frames in which these activities will be accomplished.

2. They permit the kind of accountability that allows for the maintenance of consistently high-quality service.
3. Adherence to and reliance on written policies and procedures can reduce the potential legal liability experienced by both the agencies and the individuals working within those agencies.
4. Any interagency effort, such as a comprehensive community forensic system, requires the maintenance of clear and consistent communication. These policies and procedures allow for each of the agencies and individuals involved in the provision of services to understand what has transpired prior to their involvement with the client and what is likely to (or should) occur in the future.
5. Since some degree of staff turnover is inevitable, written policies and procedures enable the various agencies to train new staff members more efficiently and successfully in their appropriate responsibilities.

Jail Services

I describe the services delivered in the jail in the same order in which an incoming inmate generally receives them. The services available in the jail include mental health screening; several kinds of mental health evaluations; outpatient crisis intervention services; psychiatric inpatient services; and case management.

Screening

Mental health screening should be required for all inmates and should occur shortly after intake. It is aimed at identifying inmates whose mental health status places them at a high risk of physical harm either to themselves or to others. Since the highest risk of suicide in a jail is during the first few hours after intake, it is imperative that this screening take place as quickly as possible.

Screening at this stage is not intended to be a complete psychological evaluation, but must (1) identify those inmates who may need a more extensive psychological evaluation; and (2) identify those individuals who, even before getting an evaluation, need special precautions to protect themselves or others.

Generally, the screening process was sound as of May 1986; in particular, the jail's intake and classification staff had gone to some trouble to research and adopt an excellent suicide risk screening form. There was, however, one exception: There was no standardized procedure to provide the results of all screenings in a timely fashion to all of the potentially interested parties throughout the jail. This is crucial, since it is similarly essential that the responses of those parties to this information be predictable and generally known.

In the Palm Beach County jail, this integrative function was being provided by one person, whose personality, memory, knowledge of the inmates, and high competence masked basic organizational flaws. Since the effective flow of information is a problem that relates to the multitude of providers and is an issue throughout the process, this issue is addressed directly later in this chapter in recommendations about the overall organization of services in jail.

Evaluation

Mental health evaluations are more extensive and detailed workups of only those inmates who have been identified in the screening process as potentially presenting serious mental health problems. These evaluations should be timely and responsive to the specific issue(s) raised during the screening. They should be completed by qualified individuals and should clearly state the criteria applied and the conclusions reached. Most of all, they should suggest implementable options for responding to whatever problems are identified.

Because of the limited resources available in any jail, it is important that mental health evaluations be only as extensive as is necessary to answer the questions. For the majority of inmates evaluated, full-scale psychological test batteries are inappropriate. Most of the questions addressed at this stage of criminal justice processing have to do with treatment or management issues, which can usually be successfully addressed by a skilled psychological interviewer. Of course, the symptoms of a small subset of individuals will present questions that can only be answered by extensive psychological testing. The need for such testing should be identified during the interview process.

The primary purpose of these evaluations must be to assist the jail personnel, as well as the various mental health service providers, in making appropriate management and treatment decisions for each inmate. Certainly, the results of these evaluations may have legal ramifications that can work for or against the legal interests of an inmate. Nonetheless, it is inappropriate for the *primary* purpose of such evaluations to be only to enable a defendant to cut his or her best legal deal.

Crisis Intervention

Crisis intervention is the primary mode of mental health service in any jail, given the length of time most inmates spend there. To be effective, crisis intervention needs to be timely. It needs to focus on the appropriate dispensing and prescription of medications. Rarely will it involve long-term verbal therapies. There will be some jail inmates who do not make bail or who are serving sentences up to 1 year, who will need somewhat longer-term types of services. However, such inmates are a distinct minority, and the general allocation of resources in the jail needs to be focused on relatively short-term crisis intervention services.

Given the complexity of providing these crisis intervention services and the multiple providers in the jail, this was the one aspect of the Palm Beach County program that we did not have adequate time to assess in May 1986. We did observe, however, that there seemed to be inadequate coordination of the various service providers in delivering the services after the screening and evaluation had been conducted.

Inpatient Services

No matter what mental health services exist in any jail, it will occasionally be necessary to place a few inmates for some limited period of time in an inpatient psychiatric setting. Obviously, the legal status of the inmate will require that this setting be secure.

It was reported to us during our site visit that this service was difficult or impossible to obtain for inmates in the Palm Beach County jail. The crisis stabilization unit then being developed under the auspices of the 45th Street Mental Health Center appeared to be capable of addressing this unmet need. In our site visit to the unit and our review of the proposed staffing pattern, we were impressed with the planning for the physical plant, both from a programming and a security standpoint. We were similarly impressed with the staffing pattern as it related to mental health needs. However, the absence of nonpatient-contact security staff to control access to and egress from the building warrants careful review.

Case Management

Case management within the jail has two distinct aspects, internal and external. As noted before, it is imperative that the various service providers, as well as the non-mental-health jail staff, keep track of the various management and treatment decisions that have been made inside the jail for each inmate during the screening, evaluation, and crisis intervention processes. This is one aspect of case management. A second aspect is linking the inmate and his or her specific mental health needs with the services the inmate requires upon leaving the jail. This second function is instrumental in helping to get the mentally ill petty offender out of the jail and into appropriate community treatment—a goal that was espoused by virtually everyone we interviewed.

The staff members currently providing both these internal and external case management services in Palm Beach County had an excellent grasp of these issues. Within the multiple-provider environment of the jail, the individuals providing these services generally seemed to do an effective job at moving information to the people who needed it. On the other hand, we heard of a number of instances in which information got "pigeonholed" in files and did not get into the hands of someone who otherwise would have been instituting services. Ultimately, then, the success of these in-jail case management and diversion efforts depends on the effectiveness of the flow of information.

In 1986, the Forensic Mental Health Services Program had two case managers who effectively carried out the external linking function from their positions and location in the 45th Street Mental Health Center. They accomplished this by spending several hours per week in the jail. Although the job definition and execution of the case management staff were most impressive, there seemed to be additional inmates who could have profited from these services and conceivably could have been released from jail if more case management resources of this type had been available.

General Considerations

This review of jail services has referred repeatedly to the issue of information flow. This issue is fundamental to the effective integration of screening, evaluation, treatment, and diversion from the jail. It appeared to us in 1986 that the effective integration of these services in Palm Beach County was significantly impeded by having multiple providers across these three services. The jail administration and the Forensic Mental Health Service Program managers needed to consider moving the responsibility and resources for the mental health services inside the jail from Emergency Medical Services, an organization providing medical services under a contract with the jail, to the managers of the program.

This observation was based on several factors. First, in order to best utilize the very expensive and limited number of hours of psychiatric service available, it would be advantageous for the psychiatrist to use the jail's psychologist to provide him or her with a summary of the relevant clinical factors regarding each patient. Similarly, the psychologist would, at times, be better able to coordinate the delivery of nonmedication services suggested by the psychiatrist. Second, this change would also be consistent with the opening of the crisis stabilization unit and might facilitate the identification and movement of appropriate patients from the jail to the unit.

We did not suggest a shift in nursing resources from the contract medical service, since the primary duties of the nurses were to continue to be medical in nature. It seemed advisable to continue the practice of using the nurses to provide the mental health screening as part of their intake medical workups, especially during evening and night shifts and during the weekends, when mental health personnel might not be present in the jail. Similarly, the contract medical service's nursing staff should continue to dispense the medications prescribed by the psychiatrist.

Another issue related to the flow of information has been discussed earlier. As long as important mental health information was provided only to the public defender's office, and was viewed by that office as strictly serving the legal interests of its clients, case management staff would continue to have difficulty in connecting inmates to appropriate community services. Ironically, this limitation on information flow could ultimately decrease the chances of such alternative dispositions being worked out. Although the public defender's office did have a strong and effective social worker assisting in dispositions involving mental health issues, it was clear that her best and most effective work could only be accomplished in conjunction with jail and Forensic Mental Health Services Program staff. Evaluations related strictly to legal issues could be accomplished by other state-supported means available to the public defender and need not be made an issue in the proper structuring and operation of the program.

Notwithstanding these recommendations, there are times when the public defender or other defense counsel will feel that it is contrary to a client's best interests to speak with mental health personnel in a nonconfidential setting. In order to avoid conflicts such as these, a simple informed consent procedure for jail mental health evaluations should be developed, preferably with the involvement of both the public defender and the state attorney's office.

A final consideration is that of how to involve program and jail mental health personnel in the routine training of correctional officers. They should be involved, and this training should focus on how and when to refer inmates for mental health services.

Court Services

Although there are only a few services and functions that are specifically attached to the court, it is impossible to overemphasize the importance of the court as the communication and decision hub of almost all of the services outlined in this chapter. Only evaluations of competency to stand trial and services aimed at providing sentencing alternatives are specifically located in the court, but all other parts of the service delivery system must relate to it.

Evaluations of Competency to Stand Trial

An evaluation of competency to stand trial is a very specific type of evaluation that answers a specific question: namely, whether the accused is psychologically able to participate in the legal process, and ultimately to receive a fair trial. As such, it relates to the court process and not specifically to the jail or community. Both the reimbursement structure and the legal orders for competency evaluations clearly indicate that performing these evaluations is a court-mandated service and falls under the auspices of the court, rather than the jail, the public defender, or the state's attorney. In most jurisdictions, a mechanism exists for both the state and the defense to obtain such evaluations without using the resources of a community forensic mental health program.

Sentencing Alternatives

Many of the people interviewed during our site visit expressed two goals as being foremost in their minds when evaluating the Forensic Mental Health Service Program: "Get 'em [clients] out and keep 'em out." In addressing these goals, the services in support of sentencing alternatives may be the most crucial part of the system. Unlike the competency evaluations described above, sentencing services relate directly to the Forensic Mental Health Services Program. They are, in fact, a solution for many of the problems identified in the jail and link the services provided inside the jail and ultimately in the community. Obviously, these services relate directly to the issues of information flow discussed above.

In 1986, there was significant room for improvement in this part of the system. Numerous examples of successful intervention were reported, but virtually all parties agreed that there was potential for a significant increase in the number of mentally ill petty offenders who could be successfully diverted. In order for this to happen, it was essential that judges, as well as the public defender and the state's attorney, receive appropriate information in a timely and usable fashion. In our view, it was the responsibility of the program staff serving the jail to insure that such reports were provided in writing and, where appropriate, were communicated by direct contact with the court. During our visit, a number of people reported that some judges felt that their needs were currently not getting met in this regard; that there were few, if any, direct contacts between the court and the people who had the appropriate information; and that in some cases, excellent sentencing recommendations were getting "buried" in file drawers, never being considered during the actual sentencing process.

*Community Treatment as a
Condition of Probation*

The use of community treatment as a condition of probation was a difficult issue in which the public defender's office and the Forensic Mental Health Services case managers appeared to have opposing and entrenched positions. There is no one right answer to this dilemma. Clearly, the public defender must pursue the best legal interests of a client. On the other hand, the use of probation conditions is often an effective tool that can significantly decrease the chances of the client again being returned to incarceration. The best resolution of this dilemma is at the individual case level. In order to serve both the interests of the client and the interests of the community, the case manager should meet with the actual defense counsel, where advisable, to balance the competing interests on a case-by-case basis.

Community Services

At virtually any point in the criminal justice sequence, an accused person can be returned to the community. Thus, a person with identified mental health needs can arrive in the community with or without legal and treatment conditions imposed by the courts. Similarly, an accused person can return to the community after a stay in the state hospital system on any of several legal statuses. In regard to identifying and providing mental health services, it does not matter very much at which point a person returns to the community. The services required will be the same. Ultimately, the ability of these clients to remain successfully in the community will depend upon the quality of the case management and the availability of the appropriate services in the community.

Case Management

As noted before, the community case management process must begin before the client is actually returned to the community. We noted with enthusiasm that the Forensic Mental Health Services caseworkers were spending several hours a week in the jail, as well as conducting occasional visits to the state inpatient forensic facility at the far end of the state. Typically, community case management services will not be of short duration. This client population typically has had both mental health and legal problems for a number of years, and it is inappropriate to think that these problems will be resolved with several months of case management or therapy. Furthermore, it is inappropriate to assume that the ultimate successful resolution of these cases is that the persons will no longer need mental health services. Many of these people are chronically and seriously mentally ill, and become engaged in the criminal justice system upon the failure of community mental health and residential services.

Ideally, successfully resolved cases should result in forensic clients becoming involved in the same service delivery system that anyone else in the community would utilize. A core element, therefore, in a comprehensive community-oriented forensic mental health program will be case managers on the forensic staff who are located in community settings and who work toward integrating forensic clients into the generic mental health, social service, and health systems.

Residential Alternatives

Case management alone, however, will not be enough. Although case management is essential for linking the client with services and for managing the predictable failures and regressions that will occur, it will be fruitless in the absence of other substantive mental health services. Particularly important for this population are residential alternatives within which specialized mental health, social, and health services can be delivered. It is also important for case managers to be aware of and skillful in obtaining appropriate entitlements for patients who may have traditionally not had access to such resources.

A glaring deficit in essential community services in Palm Beach County in 1986 was an adequate range of special residential alternatives. Obviously, it will be difficult for forensic clients to succeed in the community without having a place to live. Furthermore, access to mental health services that are generally available to the community at large is often specifically denied to forensic clients.

PLANNING PRINCIPLES

Despite the fact that the Palm Beach County Forensic Mental Health Program was developed independently of the planning principles contained in Chapter 7, it is instructive to look at the program and its development in light of those planning principles. If the principles are indeed of value, it follows that a well-conceptualized program will at the very least demonstrate attention to the same kinds of issues. Clearly, such is the case in Palm Beach County, and in the Florida Department of Health and Rehabilitative Service's published guidelines.

Principle 1. *The Mentally Disturbed Jail Inmate Must Be Viewed as a Community Issue*

Despite the narrow perspective from which many of the involved parties viewed the Forensic Mental Health Services Program, there was an almost astonishingly broad acceptance of Principle 1 by all concerned. Areas of disagreement centered not on *whether* these clients were the community's problem, but rather on *how* the community was to serve them. An impressive example of this acceptance was the willingness of the jail administration to allow a community mental health center to control an activity inside the jail itself. According to the jail administrator, this willingness came from his understanding that only by connecting his mentally ill inmates to the community and its services could he hope to get help in dealing with them. He described the jail as a consumer of the service as well as a contributor to it.

Even more important evidence of the acceptance of these clients as a community problem was the comprehensive approach taken by the two case managers, whose activities were carried out at the jail, the community mental health center offices, state hospitals, the crisis stabilization unit (soon to be opened at the time of our visit), court offices, and various sites in the community. The details of that service are described below, but the comprehensiveness with which these two case managers viewed their function was a cornerstone of the program's success. As evidence of this success, even the harshest critics of some aspects of the program had nothing but praise for the case management component of it.

Principle 2. *The Jail Is and Should Remain Primarily a Correctional Facility*

Again, the Palm Beach County program got high marks in following Principle 2, although the crisis stabilization component of the program had not been fully implemented at the time of our site visit. There was almost universal acknowledgment that the handling of the most psychotic inmates in the jail was inappropriate—a belief that was in large part intensified by some unfortunate design aspects of the jail. Despite being a relatively new building, the living areas provided very poor observation into the individual cells in which the most psychotic inmates would need to live. Narrow hallways created safety hazards to officers needing to look into these cells.

It will be interesting to see how the new crisis stabilization unit evolves. Clearly, it should enable the program to divert some very psychotic inmates charged with misdemeanors from jail. Less clear is the role to be played in treating equally psychotic inmates who are charged with serious felonies and for whom diversion may be worrisome, both to the criminal justice system and to the community. It is also likely that an aggressive strategy of brief hospitalization will prove beneficial to many such inmates, providing quick stabilization and a return to the criminal justice process. Those inmates with psychoses that are unresponsive to such stabilization will probably continue to be judged incompetent to stand trial and hospitalized in state hospital forensic settings.

Principle 3. *Serious Mental Health Needs among Inmates Require Limited But High-Quality Professional Services in Every Jail*

Principle 3 alludes to the area in which the Forensic Mental Health Services Program had both acknowledged its limitations and was searching for significant help. At the time of our site visit, the screening and evaluation components of the program also provided a significant amount of support to mentally ill inmates in the jail. Psychiatric services of a more medical nature, especially psychotropic medication, were provided by Emergency Medical Services (EMS), the medical services provider that was operating under contract with the jail. These were predictably subject to the problems commonly experienced in jail medical services. As noted above, we suggested some very specific areas in which efficiency could be increased. More important, however, is the more general issue of the role and priority of psychiatric services in the constellation of medical services available in jail.

One clear help in this regard would have been to turn over psychiatric services (i.e., the contracted psychiatrist) to the program administratively. Although the nursing services might continue necessarily to serve two masters, the psychiatrist would not. The practical result would be a better use of psychiatric time, since the communication between the existing screening agents and the psychiatrist would undoubtedly improve. Despite the problems with this aspect of the service delivery system, this function is central to the Palm Beach County program.

Principle 4. *Correctional Administrators Should Concentrate on Developing Mental Health Services in the Areas of Identification, Crisis Intervention, and Case Management at Release*

Clearly, Principle 4 best captures the need for comprehensiveness in conceptualizing a program and is among the most impressive aspects of the Palm Beach County program. Of the three, the program has demonstrated the last, case management, to have the most potential to serve both the offender and the community. As noted above, the case managers reported an astonishing reduction, nearly to zero, in the rearrest rate of their caseload. Although these were generally not seriously violent offenders, they nevertheless tended to have been arrested repeatedly, at great cost to the public budget, to police and correctional resources, to public safety, and most of all to their own lives and families.

Principle 5. *There Is No One Best Way to Organize a Jail Mental Health Program*

Although Principle 5 may have been identified as prospective, global advice to jail administrators contemplating the addition of mental health services, it has equal value to an existing program, even a very good one. Good jail mental health services are in their infancy. It is clearly not acceptable management to dismiss lightly organizational squabbles such as the one described in this chapter. As an important consumer of services of the Palm Beach County program, the public defender's needs had to be addressed. The search for creative, innovative, and flexible approaches to the clinical, political, and budgetary dilemmas involved in jail mental health can never end. The challenge to programs such as this one is simply to be willing to consider alternate structures when external conditions, systems needs, or key actors may require it, even when what is in place is exemplary and may have worked quite effectively in the past.

The Forensic Mental Health Services Program of Palm Beach County, Florida, is at the cutting edge of forensic services in the United States. In concept, it reflects the vision of the Florida Department of Health and Rehabilitation Services (1984) *Guidelines for Community Forensic Mental Health Programs.* In execution, it represents the rare integration of often competing community, county, and state interest groups. Finally, it also demonstrates how the broad planning principles that emerged from this book's study of 43 jails fit the broader context of community forensic mental health programs.

Chapter 10 ——————————————————————————

Jail Services and Community Care for the Mentally Ill in Boulder County, Colorado

Richard Warner

In each of the nation's large cities, from a quarter to a half of the men and women on skid row, in the shelters, and on the soup lines show signs of obvious psychosis (Bachrach, 1984). As Chapter 1 of this book has indicated, up to 11% of those in our city and county jails are psychotic. Thousands more pass their days devoid of purpose, segregated in large, barren boarding homes and nursing homes (Scull, 1977; Van Patten & Spar, 1979; Lamb, 1979). One estimate suggests that no more than half of the nation's schizophrenics can be living in what might be considered a domestic setting (Warner, 1985).

It is evident that our nation's overstrained mental health system has failed to meet the needs of large numbers of the seriously mentally ill, and, to a degree, has contributed to their plight. In doing so, it has also contributed to the strains on contemporary jails. Before deinstitutionalization, only a small fraction of skid row drifters in the United States were mentally ill; those with obvious features of psychosis were promptly

Richard Warner. The Mental Health Center of Boulder County, Inc., Boulder, Colorado.

picked up by the police and hospitalized (Bogue, 1963). The pioneers of community treatment in the 1950s and 1960s never intended that we should witness, in the 1970s, a large city's psychiatric system discharging nearly a quarter of its patients (from one hospital, nearly 60%) to no known address (Hopper, Baxter, & Cox, 1982).

In the face of growing problems, it has become apparent that community care for psychotic patients demands a range of support services far greater than was generally appreciated in the early decades of the deinstitutional era. Effective community support requires that the mental health agency do the following:

1. Adopt total responsibility for the severely disabled client's welfare, including helping the patient acquire such material resources as food, shelter, clothing, and medical care.
2. Aggressively pursue the client's interests—insuring that other social agencies fulfill their obligations, for example, or actively searching for patients who drop out of treatment.
3. Provide a range of supportive services that can be tailored to fit each patient's needs and that will continue as long as needed.
4. Educate the patient to live and work in the community; and provide support to family, friends, and community members.

In short, we must offer everything that the old institutions used to furnish, and a host of additional services that are essential for community tenure. To accomplish these goals begins to address some of the pressing issues of mental health services for jail inmates, in that they can help prevent arrest in the first place; furthermore, it demonstrates how one of our basic principles of planning jail mental health services, defining the jail as a community problem, actually operates in practice.

BACKGROUND

The population of Boulder County, Colorado, is approximately 210,000 people, about 90,000 of whom live in the city of Boulder.

The county extends westward into the front range of the Rocky Mountains and eastward into the farming and ranching country of the Great Plains. Major local employers include computer-manufacturing companies, governmental scientific establishments, and the University of Colorado. The county jail, which has been considered a national model correctional facility, is operated by the sheriff's department. In 1986, the daily census of the jail averaged 167 inmates. The Mental Health Center of Boulder County employs nearly 200 part-time and full-time staff and offers comprehensive inpatient, outpatient, and emergency psychiatric services county-wide. The center sees about 4,000 clients each year, with over 1,800 being in active treatment at any one time.

For the past decade, the Mental Health Center has provided on-site psychiatric evaluation and treatment services to the Boulder County jail, with the primary goal of preventing the inappropriate incarceration of seriously mentally ill people. Although these services are useful and important, they would be ineffective in achieving their goal if they were not part of a comprehensive program for the treatment and support of psychotic patients. Unless adequate community and hospital treatment programs are established, people suffering from psychosis tend to accumulate in jail. This chapter, therefore, focuses not only on the Mental Health Center's jail services, but also on the agency's community support system for the seriously mentally ill.

The community support system of the Mental Health Center of Boulder County has been built on the premise that psychotic patients should not remain in degrading and nontherapeutic environments. In Boulder County, the Mental Health Center places no physically healthy, functional psychotics in nursing homes. The administrators of the center have actively discouraged local nursing home operators from opening wards for chronically ill psychiatric patients, arguing that nursing homes cannot provide an adequate quality of care and environment for such patients. In Boulder County there are no boarding homes housing the mentally ill (though there is a cheap hotel where a few clients stay), and when patients are found living on the streets or in an emergency shelter, efforts are made to accommodate them in one of the residential facilities described below.

PHILOSOPHY AND GOALS

A basic element of the philosophy that motivated the Mental Health Center personnel to develop on-site jail psychiatric services is one that has been discussed earlier in this book as Principle 1: "The mentally ill jail inmate must be viewed as a community issue." Treatment of the mentally ill, regardless of whether they are in jail or not, is seen as part of a community mental health center's job. In the jail or in the community, the Mental Health Center's services in Boulder County are directed as a priority toward psychotic patients and others with severe levels of disturbance.

The principal goal of the jail outreach program is to transfer from the jail to treatment settings severely disturbed people who are inappropriately incarcerated. Many psychotic people are jailed for offenses that result directly from their disordered thinking or from the poverty that is the product of their illness. Stressful jail conditions often worsen the symptoms of psychosis in these inmates. Schizophrenia, for example, is an illness that has been shown to be reactive to a variety of stresses and environmental effects (Warner, 1985). My colleagues and I believe, therefore, that it is preferable to treat psychotic people outside the jail in an appropriate mental health setting whenever possible. As emphasized earlier in this book, jails are primarily correctional facilities; they are ill suited to provide treatment for severe psychiatric disorders.

It is true that some psychotic patients improve upon admission to jail, because they are removed from the harmful effects of drug and alcohol abuse or from the stresses of lack of food and shelter that the homeless endure. However, we do not consider this an argument for treating such people in jail; rather, it suggests the need for finding adequate, protective treatment settings and community support for the mentally ill. Confronting the needs of such jail inmates has pushed the Mental Health Center of Boulder County to expand its range of treatment programs for the severely disturbed. Mental health professionals sometimes argue that the "structure" of the jail is reassuring to psychotic patients. If this is so, then we would see it as an argument for providing treatment settings with this kind of structure, not for leaving the mentally ill in a correctional institution that is otherwise ill adapted to their needs. Correctional personnel, in fact, generally report that psychotic inmates often respond poorly to the usual institutional controls, and may spend much of their period of incarceration in solitary confinement.

We are cautious in using the argument that a mentally ill offender should remain in jail in order to "learn the consequences of his or her actions." Many psychotic people do not learn from this experience, but are jailed repeatedly for the same offenses. We have found that it is generally more productive if the consequence of such a person's crime is a period of treatment as a condition of probation or suspended sentence, rather than a jail term.

PROGRAM STAFFING

Two Mental Health Center staff members, a mental health worker and a psychiatrist, spend some time each week in the Boulder County jail providing regular evaluation and treatment services to jail inmates. The mental health worker is an experienced clinician capable of performing evaluations independently, forming treatment plans, and making recommendations to judges and lawyers. This position has usually been filled by someone with a master's degree in psychiatric nursing, social work, or psychology. The mental health worker spends up to 10 hours a week on jail-related duties, attending the facility on two occasions a week and providing telephone consultation at other times. The psychiatrist accompanies the mental health worker to the jail on one occasion each week, providing about 3 hours of service.

In addition to these regularly scheduled services, an acutely disturbed inmate may be seen at any time by a mental health professional from the center's emergency services team. The emergency services worker will perform an on-site evaluation whenever requested by jail personnel, consult with a center psychiatrist, and make recommendations to the correctional staff and judge regarding treatment or transfer to a treatment setting.

SCREENING AND REFERRAL

Screening for mental health problems is performed by the correctional staff. Evidence of abnormal mood, behavior, or thinking is reported to the jail nurse by officers in the booking and living areas. After evaluating the inmate's condition, the nurse may contact the mental health staff immediately or at the time of the next regularly scheduled contact. A severe level of disturbance requiring isolation of the inmate, a suicide attempt, or serious suicidal ideas would all be indications for an immediate referral to the emergency psychiatric service.

Once a week, the center's mental health worker and psychiatrist meet with the jail nursing staff, the jail psychologist, and the psychologist from the county department of community corrections, who is responsible for providing pretrial mental health evaluation reports to the court. At this meeting, the Mental Health Center personnel identify those inmates who are most in need of psychiatric evaluation and treatment, based on information provided by jail and community corrections staff. The arrest record is often consulted for details of the offense leading to incarceration and for evidence of mental illness (or, in some instances, of grounds for involuntary treatment).

Mental Health Center staff members are principally seeking referrals of inmates who may need to be transferred to a treatment setting outside the jail, and of cases of psychiatric disorder that require skilled psychiatric diagnostic evaluation or that may benefit from the use of psychotropic medication. As Principal 3 in Chapter 7 notes, "Serious mental health needs among inmates require limited but high-quality professional services in every jail." Such inmates include those with psychosis, organic brain disorders, or serious mood disturbance, or those for whom the possibility of a serious disorder has been raised but not confirmed.

One type of mental disorder is worthy of special mention, as it may easily be overlooked. Among jail inmates, mental health staff often locate people with explosive and violent behavior, volatile moods, and poor attention and concentration, who were hyperactive as children and may have been treated with stimulants at that time to control their behavior. Such people are often found to suffer from an adult form of attention deficit disorder; if they are treated with a stimulant such as Ritalin, their behavior, self-control, concentration, and learning ability may improve significantly. The Mental Health Center team encourages the referral of such inmates, since treatment produces obvious benefits for the persons' behavior both inside the jail and upon return to the community.

Referrals are sought from other sources besides the correctional staff. An inmate's attorney may request a recommendation to the court about possible future treatment, or the court may order such an evaluation. If a recently admitted inmate is already in treatment at the Mental Health Center, his or her outpatient therapist may ask the jail team to evaluate the inmate's condition and make treatment suggestions. In some cases, relatives or friends may call the Mental Health Center suggesting that we see an inmate in order to initiate treatment. Before conducting any evaluation, Mental Health Center personnel explain to the person the reason for the interview, specifying who has requested it and to whom information will be given. When necessary, the inmate is asked to sign a form giving permission for the release of information to relevant people and agencies.

ASSESSMENT AND TREATMENT

Evaluation of a mentally disordered inmate usually requires that a substantial amount of information be gathered, beyond that which is available from the interview with the client. Mental health staff will review the arrest record and other criminal justice information; obtain clinical information from psychiatric records, contacting prior treatment agencies where necessary; and call relatives or others in the community for background information on the inmate's behavior, social functioning, and past history. Jail admission may indicate that community treatment for an inmate's mental illnesses has been unsuccessful, and it offers an opportunity to assess and revise the previous treatment plan. Some mentally ill inmates will not have been in treatment recently, and an assessment will need to be made of the prior course of the illness and future treatment needs.

An effort is made to evaluate all inmates who are believed to be suffering from psychosis. If a psychotic inmate refuses to see the mental health staff, correctional personnel may seek a court order allowing the evaluation to proceed. If someone is found to be suffering from an acute or fairly severe degree of mental illness, it is likely that the mental health team will recommend transfer to a treatment setting for voluntary or involuntary treatment. The treatment facility may be locked or unlocked.

The members of the jail mental health team recognize that many of the mentally ill offenders they see should be considered answerable for their crimes. In most cases in which an offender is released to a treatment setting, charges are not dropped. The offender is released on bond and returns to court to answer the charges after a period of treatment. In those instances in which a mentally ill offender is not acutely disturbed and his or her crime is not a product of disordered thinking, the individual is likely to remain in jail and to receive treatment there.

Many of the mentally ill people who are transferred to treatment settings from the jail require involuntary treatment. The Colorado Mental Illness Statute allows for such involuntary treatment of offenders, provided that criminal charges are temporarily placed in abeyance. Criminal proceedings resume when a person is no longer in involuntary treatment. Very often, the crime that has led to the mentally ill person's being detained in jail, if it is a direct result of the illness, is in itself sufficient grounds for involuntary treatment, as it may indicate that the person is gravely disabled or a danger to others as a result of mental disorder. If the mentally ill inmate has committed a serious offense, it may not be advisable to place the charges in abeyance or to transfer him or her out of a secure facility. In these cases, if the person's condition is severe enough, transfer to a forensic psychiatric hospital is recommended.

According to this approach, the only psychotic people remaining in jail should be (1) those who refuse treatment and are too mildly disturbed to meet the criteria for involuntary psychiatric treatment; (2) those awaiting trial for offenses that are too severe to allow the persons to be released from a correctional facility; and (3) those whose mental illness is under good control and whose crimes are unrelated to their illness. These psychotic people (and, we may hope, only these) will be monitored and, where possible, treated in the jail itself. Under no circumstances do we treat in the jail a person with a severe, acute, agitated psychosis requiring isolation or restraints. Such a person should be transferred immediately to a hospital unit for treatment.

Arranging the timely transfer of the mentally ill to treatment settings is facilitated by the familiar working relationship between mental health personnel and the criminal justice system. In part, this familiarity is a result of the relatively small size of the county population (210,000) and the county agencies. Mental health personnel may walk from the jail down the hall to the judge's chambers and make a recommendation to the judge about the disposition of an inmate or leave a message with the judge's clerk. Similarly, recommendations for treatment are readily passed to community corrections or probation personnel, who will present them at the next appropriate court hearing. This procedure allows Mental Health Center staff to avoid spending significant amounts of time in court—a commitment that would be beyond the resources of the center.

Treatment recommendations are not uncommonly the product of negotiations among mental health staff, attorneys, and probation officers. An inmate's attorney, for example, may argue for involuntary hospital treatment for his or her client under the Colorado Mental Illness Statute, rather than longer-term admission to the forensic unit of the state hospital. In another case, the district attorney may object to community placement of an offender with a history of assault, or the Mental Health Center may not wish to assume responsibility for the community treatment of a violent, psychotic person as a condition of probation unless the terms of the probation specify immediate arrest if the offender drops out of treatment. The complexity of these issues requires that members of the mental health staff be sufficiently trained and experienced to function independently, and that they have direct access to Mental Health Center administrators when policy decisions are called for.

For those patients who receive treatment while they remain in jail, progress is monitored by the jail nurses daily and by members of the mental health team during their regular visits. Records are maintained at both the Mental Health Center and the jail. Jail medical and psychiatric records are confidential and are not made available to criminal justice personnel. If an inmate was already in Mental Health Center treatment before being booked into the jail, the outpatient therapist will be kept informed of the patient's progress while in custody. If the inmate is not already in treatment, a referral to outpatient care, where indicated, will be made while the inmate is incarcerated, and the treatment initiated in jail will be continued after release.

A jail nurse joins the mental health team for all inmate interviews and evaluations. This procedure insures, on the one hand, that the mental health team is fully aware of inmate management difficulties and the available evidence of mental illness. On the other hand, the nurses get detailed information concerning the nature of each inmate's diagnosis, treatment, and eventual disposition. In addition, the nurses refine their psychiatric evaluation skills, learn which aspects of the patient's condition to monitor as treatment progresses, and become skilled in making decisions about which cases to refer to the Mental Health Center as urgent or routine cases. This practice of combining correctional and mental health staffs has thus proved valuable for screening, referral, evaluation, treatment planning, inmate monitoring, staff training, and interagency liaisons.

INTENSIVE RESIDENTIAL TREATMENT

Many of the mentally ill people evaluated in the Boulder
County jail are transferred directly to an intensive residential
treatment unit, Cedar House. This type of component has not
been discussed very much in this book, but should be considered
a crucial element for the successful conduct of the case management services discussed in Chapter 7. Cedar House is a large
house for 15 psychiatric patients operated by the Mental Health
Center of Boulder County in a residential and business district
of the city of Boulder. It functions principally as an alternative
to a psychiatric hospital and in part as a halfway house. Like a
psychiatric hospital, it offers all the usual diagnostic and treatment services; however, these services cost less than a third as
much as private hospital treatment, and thus it is feasible for
patients to remain for long periods if necessary. Usually admitted with some kind of acute psychiatric problem (most often an
acute psychotic relapse), clients may stay anywhere from a day
to a year or more. However, the average period is about 12 days.
The availability of this cheaper alternative to standard hospital
care substantially improves the center's ability to transfer seriously disturbed inmates out of the jail.

Unlike a psychiatric hospital, Cedar House is noncoercive.
No patient can be strapped down, locked in, or medicated un-
willingly. Staff members must encourage patients to comply
voluntarily with treatment requirements and house rules. The
people who cannot be managed are those who repeatedly walk
away or run away and those who are violent. Since the alternative for patients who are unable to stay at Cedar House is
hospital treatment, which very few prefer, the large majority of
residents accept the necessary restrictions. Few patients need to
be transferred to a hospital. In practice, most clients with schizophrenia or psychotic depression can be treated at Cedar House
through all phases of their illness, and many patients with acute
mania can also be managed successfully. There is little doubt
that a large number of the people treated in this residential
facility would be subjected to coercive measures, such as re-

straints or seclusion, if they were admitted to a hospital where such approaches are available and routinely used.

The environment is deliberately styled to be similar to that of a middle-class home, not a hospital. The floors are carpeted; a fire burns in the hearth; a cat curls up in the most comfortable chair; shelves of books are available. Residents and visitors come and go fairly freely. Staff and patients interact casually, eat together, and are encouraged to treat one another with mutual respect. The goal is to allow therapists and clients alike to retain their dignity and humanity and to foster cooperation.

Residential treatment of this intensity requires a staffing pattern similar to that of a hospital. A mental health worker and a nurse are on duty at all times. On weekdays, three experienced therapists (one of them half-time) work with the patients. A psychiatrist is present for 3 hours a day; a team leader directs the program; and a secretarial assistant manages the office work and the purchasing of household supplies. The treatment setting calls for staff members who are tolerant and empathic and it brings out their capacity to find inventive solutions to difficult problems independently.

There is no commonly used form of psychiatric treatment or diagnostic measure that cannot be provided for residents of this treatment facility (except for electroconvulsive therapy). Patients with acute or chronic organic brain disorders, for example, can be evaluated using the laboratories and diagnostic equipment of local hospitals. Consulting physicians provide treatment for medical problems.

An essential step in the treatment of a patient entering Cedar House is the evaluation of the patient's social system. What has happened to bring this patient in for treatment at this particular time? What are his or her financial circumstances, living arrangements, and work situation? Have there been recent changes? Are there family tensions? From the answers to such questions as these, a plan may be made that will (we hope) diminish the chances of relapse or jail admission after the patient leaves residential treatment.

Although much cheaper than hospital care, Cedar House is

still a relatively expensive program. The required level of staffing imposes high fixed costs, which cannot be reduced without seriously altering the nature of the program. Such costs would not be justifiable for an agency with a small catchment area (much below 200,000 persons). With the fixed costs of Cedar House, as available funding decreases, cuts have to be made instead in outpatient services and other parts of the community support system, with consequent deterioration in continuity of care. In these circumstances, the risk emerges of creating a new type of revolving-door patient—one who repeatedly re-enters the residential community facility.

OUTPATIENT SERVICES

The broader system of outpatient services is available to persons after their release from the jail. In fact, in order to improve services to the most severely disturbed psychotics and to decrease the revolving-door phenomenon, the Mental Health Center of Boulder County established a team in 1983 that offers intensive community care. Therapists on this community support team have small caseloads of about 15 clients. The team is responsible for approximately 70 of the most difficult-to-treat patients out of a total of about 350 psychotics currenting being treated by the center's teams. The remaining, less severely disturbed psychotic patients are treated on outpatient teams by therapists with caseloads of about 40 clients. Patients assigned to the new community support team are those who tend to relapse frequently and who appear to be most in need of the special services provided by the team. These services include a day care program; therapist contact several times a week when needed; money management; home visiting; emergency intervention; daily monitoring of medication; and placement in one of the center's supervised apartments or halfway house. The team operates out of a large old house (formerly a fraternity house); because it is separate from the center's main outpatient offices, the patients may use the building fairly freely as a drop-in facility.

A therapist often has to give a good deal of assistance with budgeting, and, in many cases, actually manages a patient's money. Controlling the patient's money decreases the likelihood that he or she will commit a minor crime such as "defrauding an innkeeper" because of having spent the whole month's Social Security payment early. Limiting the amount of money available each day is also a way of decreasing daily drug and alcohol abuse in those cases where this has proved to be a problem.

Establishing a team with a special mission, and assigning to it therapists who have a particular interest in treating psychotic patients with high probabilities of police contacts, have eased many of the staffing problems commonly encountered in treating this population of patients. Members of this team have had little difficulty in abandoning the traditional 50-minute therapy session, and in developing flexible and innovative responses to their clients' crises. Team members provide support for one another in working with very demanding clients, and they are able to establish reasonable goals for progress in treatment that are substantially different from the expectations of outpatient therapists on teams treating less disturbed patients.

SUPERVISED APARTMENTS

An important function of the community support team is to manage the center's long-established system of supervised and rent-subsidized housing. The unemployed psychotic, unless living with his or her family, is likely to reside in a seedy, low-rent room, a boarding home, or a nursing home. Persons with histories of mental illness who are released from local jails often find suitable housing the most difficult aspect of successfully remaining in the community. This situation has been noted in Chapter 9 on the Palm Beach County, Florida, program. Many of these individuals, having fallen ill early in life, have little experience of independent living; some have poor judgment and lack the capacity to manage a household. For such people, supervised housing is a necessity.

Many agencies have demonstrated that cooperative apartments work well for chronically ill patients who are leaving hospitals after several years of residence (Sandall, Hawley, & Gordon, 1975), but until recently, such group homes have less commonly proved viable for younger psychotic patients who have not spent years in an institution. These patients, who are generally more volatile, subject to relapse, and likely to abuse drugs and alcohol, require a more intensive level of supervision. In the Boulder supervised living program, staff members hold house meetings for residents at least once a week in their apartments, in addition to providing other outpatient services. Help with household management often involves sorting out problems with "crashers" (i.e., uninvited guests) or disputes over household chores.

More than 40 center patients live in supervised apartments in Boulder County. For many psychotics, living alone is the best arrangement, because the stresses of cooperative living may provoke relapse; others find loneliness to be a major problem. Supervised apartments in Boulder range in size from one- to eight-person households. At some of the larger homes, a university student is hired to live in (rent-free) and to provide some supervision in the evenings. These larger homes can accommodate clients who have more limited capacity for independent living. Supplying increasing amounts of staff support on the premises has made it possible to develop a range of community living arrangements, up to the level of the traditional, staffed halfway house, for clients with progressively lower levels of functioning.

HOSPITAL BEDS

Paradoxically, one of the most crucial elements in a community support system is the psychiatric hospital. However comprehensive the community programs may be, there will remain a handful of patients who cannot be cared for outside of a hospital. A few patients consistently refuse treatment and will always walk away from an open-door establishment; a few become violent and fail to respond to the usual form of treatment, representing a danger to mental health staff and members of the public. Some psychotics exacerbate their condition by making frequent use of hallucinogens or alcohol or by inhaling volatile solvents. When even the best-supervised community placements fail, these patients are likely to end up in jail or on the street; but the effort to help them will have put an immense strain on the community support system. Many hours of work will have been put into makeshift treatment plans that have little hope of success.

Recognizing that the severely restricted access to state hospital beds was creating major problems of this type, the administrators of the Mental Health Center of Boulder County and other county mental health centers negotiated in 1983 with the Colorado Division of Mental Health to allocate state hospital beds to each county on an equitable basis. The resulting arrangement has proved highly beneficial. County mental health centers now work closely with the state hospital to use their limited number of beds to best effect. The number of psychotics in the Boulder County jail has been drastically reduced. At any time, the number of adult patients from the Mental Health Center of Boulder County in state or private hospitals is about 15 to 20. About 8 of these patients will be long-term inpatients who will be hospitalized for over a year. The remainder are medium- and short-stay patients, who remain from a few days to a few months. Clearly, the number of psychotics who need long-term hospital care is small—fewer than 3% of the 350 or so functionally psychotic patients enrolled at the Mental Health Center— but it is of prime importance for the community that this level of care be available.

CONCLUSION

The provision of adequate hospital and community treatment services for the mentally ill is essential whenever we wish to minimize problems arising from the presence of mentally ill people in local jails. Recognizing that the mentally ill jail inmate is a community issue is a necessary prerequisite to building these treatment programs and to developing cooperative mental health evaluation and treatment services in the local jail.

Chapter 11 ————————————————————————

A Practical Guide for Mental Health Service Providers in Local Jails

Judith F. Cox, Gerald Landsberg, and M. Peter Paravati

As is clearly evident from the preceding chapters, mental health professionals who provide services to jail inmates face a very challenging task. In some ways, these clinicians are pioneers, in that they are operating within a system that has traditionally been closed to outside community involvement. As has been indicated in Chapter 5, this history does not mean that conflict between the mental health staff and the correctional staff is inevitable. The basic goals for the mental health services that the two staffs share far outweigh the day-to-day irritations. Nonetheless, friction will almost certainly develop if mental health personnel inadvertently obstruct jail operations or violate regulations that are essential for the orderly management of the facility. This chapter, which concludes the book on a most

Judith F. Cox. New York State Office of Mental Health, Albany, New York.
Gerald Landsberg. Ulster County Mental Health Center, Kingston, New York.
M. Peter Paravati. New York State Commission on Corrections, Albany, New York.

concrete note, has been written to help the novice mental health professional avoid problems of this sort. Specifically, this chapter describes a variety of potentially troublesome situations that clinicians can routinely expect to encounter while working in county and municipal jails. It also offers several suggestions to help clinicians deliver mental health services more effectively within these local corrections systems.

GENERAL SECURITY AND ATTITUDINAL ISSUES

In most jurisdictions, state law clearly establishes that responsibility for the overall safety and welfare of inmates rests with the chief jail administrator. Staff and inmate safety can be assured only if facility operations are conducted in a secure environment. Consequently, security will almost always have a higher priority than mental health treatment or any other program activity. This hierarchy of goals remains constant, regardless of whether the services are provided at the jail or at an external mental health or medical program site.

"Security" in this context refers to those methods and procedures that are used to maintain order within the institution and to prevent escapes. It encompasses such diverse activities as the supervision and transportation of inmates, the development and enforcement of regulations for visits to inmates, and the control of contraband articles (e.g., weapons and drugs).

Efforts made by different parties to accomplish specific mental health and security objectives are by no means mutually exclusive. Clinicians who have a thorough understanding of the nature of jails and the way that jails operate will be able to serve inmates far more effectively.

Clinicians should understand that working in a jail is not the same as working in a more conventional mental health environment. Clients are often suspected of committing serious crimes, and working in a jail can be an intimidating experience. These places are often poorly lighted, inadequately ventilated, and crowded with unsavory-appearing people. Mental health personnel must honestly address their fears, attitudes, and biases about treating clients, some of whom have been or are violent, in a closed setting. Those who feel that they will not be able to work with inmates in an objective manner and to advocate on their behalf for appropriate services when necessary should speak openly with their supervisors regarding these reservations. Core problems in this regard may be addressed by more training or consultation with senior colleagues, but they must be recognized and dealt with honestly. If these concerns still seem insurmountable, mental health professionals should not be reluctant to admit that they cannot function in the correctional environment.

ESTABLISHING LIAISONS AND MAINTAINING EFFECTIVE RELATIONSHIPS

Before any effective services can be delivered to inmates, mental health professionals must first establish good working relationships with facility administrators and representatives of other key criminal justice agencies. Many problems can be avoided if these officials support mental health program goals and understand the limitations of mental health interventions.

Mental health personnel will not be able to establish a useful rapport with jail authorities if they convey the impression that they see their role primarily as one of monitoring the facility, reporting abuses, and acting exclusively as inmate advocates. Rather, mental health care can and should be represented as an integral support service within the normal operating constraints of the jail environment.

Mental health clinicians will also need a good relationship with line correctional staff. Line correctional personnel are the people who make the facility run smoothly on a day-to-day basis. These individuals are referred to as "officers," not "guards." There is a significant difference in the job performed by a person responsible for the safe operation of a correctional facility (an officer) and the job performed by someone who watches valuable objects to deter thieves (a guard). Obviously, personnel from outside the jail will experience an array of problems if they alienate the officers or shift supervisors. Mental health workers are dependent upon these officials for assistance in entering and exiting the facility, summoning inmates, obtaining valuable information regarding an inmate's behavior or background, and obtaining access to a suitable conference room or telephone. Officers can do a great deal to keep inconveniences to a minimum.

Clinicians should be sensitive to the organizational command within the local correctional facility. They must understand both the formal and informal hierarchies, as well as the accepted routes for the flow of routine management information and complaints. It is highly recommended that clinicians ask the chief facility administrator to designate a principal liaison officer with whom they can regularly discuss operational needs and problems. They must insure that they are not seen as "going behind the backs" of key members of the safety staff. The person who may be most effective in this liaison role is the shift commander.

Relationships with jail medical personnel are very important as well. Jails are required by most state codes to employ a physician on at least a part-time basis, and many employ full-time nurses or physician's assistants. Mental health personnel should speak regularly with the jail medical staff to exchange information on matters such as inmates' mental status, behavioral manifestations, and reactions to psychotropic medication, in order to avoid possible conflicts over issues involving treatment (e.g., the need for psychiatric hospitalization) and to insure continuity of care.

Finally, mental health staff should cultivate a good working relationship with local judges, the district attorney's office, and members of the county probation and parole departments. These relationships are necessary to facilitate certain inpatient admissions and to arrange alternatives to incarceration for a particular client. Prior to establishing these relationships, however, clinicians should consult with their local mental health director or commissioner to determine the appropriate process of coordination.

Attempts to improve professional relationships between correctional and mental health staffs will be greatly facilitated if a special effort is made to maintain clear and open lines of communication. Conflict between correctional and mental health personnel can easily occur if neither side understands the other's responsibilities and limitations or if disagreements over the handling of individual cases are not adequately discussed. Misunderstandings commonly arise, for example, when correctional personnel conclude that a certain inmate requires inpatient psychiatric care. The inmate may not meet the criteria for hospitalization, but detention officials will probably direct their anger and frustration toward the evaluating clinician if it is not made clear why the person cannot be hospitalized. All such cases should be discussed as they arise, along with any problems that mental health personnel encounter while providing inmate services. Jail and mental health staffs will not always agree, but it is better to address the issue directly in an effort to explore possible solutions than to let the anger simmer until a major confrontation is unavoidable.

ENTERING AND EXITING THE FACILITY

All jails have a formal process that must be followed when visitors enter and exit the facility. In most jails, mental health personnel do not work for the sheriff and must thus follow many of the rules that apply to visitors, even though these personnel are working in the jail. Upon entering the jail, members of the mental health staff will probably have to check in, obtain an appropriate pass, and sign a log in accordance with established procedures. Proper identification often must be presented as well.

Most correctional administrators will not allow anyone entering the jail to carry sharp instruments, cameras, tape recorders, or other items that potentially threaten the security of the institution. Occasionally, jail policy may require that clinicians step through a metal detector or remove all contents of their pockets, handbags, or briefcases for inspection.

A clinician getting ready to leave the facility should remember to sign out, return the visitor's pass if one was issued, and follow any other required procedures. It is interesting to note that many of these procedures are the inverse of what happens in a hospital emergency room where a police officer brings in a person for psychiatric evaluation. In that setting, hospital policies and medical practices dictate where the officer is allowed to sit, what he or she signs, whether the weapons must be checked, and so on.

FACILITY RULES

Legal codes in many states mandate that local correctional facilities give each incoming prisoner a written copy of facility rules and information about such matters as rules of conduct, items that inmates are allowed to have in their possession, and the nature of available health services. Clinicians should obtain copies of these rules and familiarize themselves with all regulations pertaining to staff members who work in the jail. Facility officials should be approached to answer any questions about these issues.

Specific regulations vary from jail to jail. Mental health personnel should always check with the shift commander when they are uncertain about the propriety of a given activity or inmate request. It is important to keep in mind that something that appears to be an innocent favor (e.g., mailing a letter for an inmate) may actually be illegal. Under no circumstances should a clinician accept gifts from inmates, offer gifts, or transport items for clients outside the jail.

SCHEDULING SERVICES

When scheduling services for jail inmates, clinicians must take the timing of regular facility activities into consideration. Mental health personnel should review the daily schedule and be prepared to avoid or work around interruptions or distractions such as the following:

1. *Inmate counts.* State codes and regulations usually require the jail staff to conduct an actual count of the entire inmate population at least once during every regularly scheduled shift. No movement is permitted in the jail during this time.

2. *Meals.* Meal times tend to be very structured and inflexible in correctional facilities as well as in other institutions. An inmate who receives mental health services while meals are being served many lose his or her opportunity to eat. Many facilities serve lunch and dinner much earlier than is common in the regular community.

3. *Shift changes.* Officers change shifts three times a day. Most jails do not allow anyone to enter the jail until the shift change has been completed. At best, a clinician arriving at this time will almost certainly encounter a delay in getting an inmate escorted to an interview room while incoming officers receive their assignments. Day and evening shift changes are typically scheduled to take place during 7:00 and 8:00 A.M. and between 3:00 and 4:00 P.M..

4. *Court appearances.* Before going to see a particular inmate, it is wise to determine whether he or she has a court appearance scheduled. A court appearance will obviously take priority over a mental health session.

5. *Visitation.* Inmates' visits should not be interrupted if at all possible. If there is a regularly scheduled day for visitation, it is preferable to schedule mental health appointments for another time. Attorneys and probation officers, however, do not always go to the jail during normal visiting hours. A clinician should not be offended if an inmate prefers to see an attorney, if one happens to arrive at the same time as the clinician. From the typical inmate's point of view, legal services are much more important than mental health treatment.

6. *Recreation.* In many states, prisoners confined in local correctional facilities are entitled to some minimum amount of recreation each day. Though inmates can be removed from recreation, mental health personnel will be more readily accepted by both inmates and the correctional staff if they avoid recreation time for inmate consultations. Inmates usually look

forward to recreation because it provides one of their few opportunities to leave the tier, exercise, and speak freely with their peers.

In addition to the considerations mentioned above, mental health staff members working part-time should make a deliberate effort to be at the jail on the same days and at the same time every week. A standard routine lets jail officials know when the clinicians will be available, and enables them to schedule inmate appointments and staff consultations accordingly.

PROVIDING MENTAL HEALTH SERVICES

It is generally recommended that mental health personnel wear attire that is businesslike and professional in nature rather than casual. In addition, clinicians should be careful not to carry large sums of money or wear valuable jewelry when visiting the jail.

Many jails are old, and the physical conditions of the available interview rooms frequently leave much to be desired. Mental health personnel should nevertheless object if the space reserved for their use is grossly inadequate (e.g., is unsafe, lacks privacy, etc.). For most interviews, a private room with see-through windows is ideal. The room should not be totally soundproof when the door is closed, however, because assistance may be needed if an inmate becomes violent or otherwise unmanageable. Mental health staff members should request that an officer remain nearby if they are at all concerned about an inmate's behavior.

Most inmates respect and willingly cooperate with mental health personnel. A few, however, are overtly hostile to anyone in a position of authority. Mental health personnel assigned to a jail do not have to tolerate insults, rudeness, or other forms of verbal abuse. Inmates should be confronted when their behavior is no longer within acceptable limits, and any physical threat should be reported immediately to security officers.

Community-based clients sometimes try to use their relationship with mental health personnel for purposes that are unrelated to legitimate therapeutic needs. Inmates similarly try on occasion to take advantage of clinicians assigned to the jail. They do so for a number of reasons: Some may become bored and want attention; others will present certain symptoms in the hope of obtaining a better cell assignment, privileges, or medication. Mental health personnel need not be cynical or overly suspicious of inmates' behavior and requests, but it is important to remember that the potential for manipulation always exists.

Mental health staff members cannot assume that every jail inmate who needs treatment will be referred for a formal assessment. Correction officers refer those individuals who have the most difficulty adjusting, but many symptoms of mental illness that would be apparent to a clinician may be overlooked or misinterpreted by someone who has not had comparable training. Even if inmates are encouraged to request mental health appointments for themselves, many will be reluctant to do so because of peer pressure to maintain a macho, stoic facade. In addition to screening all referrals, therefore, clinicians should consider initiating informal contacts with other inmates on the tiers. The additional effort may result in the identification of inmates in need of special care. Periodic visits on the tier can also help the clinicians gain credibility in the eyes of both inmates and correctional personnel.

Interviews conducted outside the jail pose special security problems. Depending upon the characteristics of the room being used and the background of the individual to be seen, officers may be reluctant to remove a prisoner's handcuffs even if mental health personnel request the officers to do so. Clinicians should keep in mind that the officers have probably spent a considerable amount of time with the inmate and often are a good source of information about the individual's recent levels of violence. Mental health personnel may want to discuss security needs and expectations with jail officials prior to an inmate's appointment, in order to avoid any last-minute confusion. Clinicians should also make a private waiting room available if they are unexpectedly delayed, so as not to frighten other clients or embarrass the inmate.

TREATMENT GOALS

Establishing realistic treatment goals for the mentally ill inmate is often a difficult task. Prisoners tend to remain in custody for very brief periods of time. The average length of stay for jail inmates is 11 days, with many remaining incarcerated for less than a week.

Treatment planning for nonsentenced jail inmates is especially complicated, because it is often nearly impossible to predict how long they will remain in custody. Even the prisoners themselves may not know whether or when they are going to be released. Charges may be suddenly dismissed; bail may be lowered to an amount that an individual can afford; or a plea bargain may be reached that results in an inmate's immediate transfer to state prison. Alternatively, the issue of the inmate's competency or responsibility may become the primary factor determining his or her immediate future.

When establishing treatment goals for jail clients, mental health personnel should consider both the inmates' immediate treatment needs and what can be reasonably accomplished during the inmates' incarceration. As has been detailed in Chapter 7, the primary treatment goals for jail inmates will usually be crisis stabilization and maintenance at an appropriate level of functioning while in custody. Mental health staff members should keep in mind, however, that the inmates' living area is frequently antitherapeutic in nature. Cell blocks tend to be crowded and noisy; there is little or no privacy; and correction officers have total control over nearly all aspects of the inmates' lives. These conditions can obviously aggravate certain mental illnesses. Clinicians may wish to take these factors into consideration when developing treatment plans or when assessing the amount of progress that a client should be making.

Again, consistent with the planning principles articulated in Chapter 7, clinicians should also try to develop release-planning goals for the jail inmate that will link the individual to an appropriate community-based mental health program and will be congruent with the restrictions that the court imposes on the client. Like the discharge-planning process at a psychiatric hospital, release planning should be initiated during a clinician's early contacts with an inmate. Release planning (particularly linkage with a formal treatment program) is especially critical for inmates who receive psychotropic medications and who will have a continued need for this type of therapy after release.

The mental health staff should develop more comprehensive release-planning goals for inmates with relatively long sentences. In the larger jails, counselors are sometimes available to help clinicians arrange these community program linkages. If resources permit, treatment goals focusing on personal growth should also be established. However, it is worth reiterating that only short-term goals are realistic for the vast majority of inmates.

List of Participating Sites

Location	Facility	Sheriff (1981)
Akron, OH	Summit County Jail	David Troutman
Albuquerque, NM	Bernilillo County Detention Center	Michael Hanrahan[1]
Billerica, MA	Middlesex County Jail and House of Correction	John Buckley
Biloxi, MS	Harrison County Jail	Howard Hobbs
Binghamton, NY	Broome County Jail	Anthony Ruffo
Bloomington, IL	McLean County Law and Justice Center	Steven Brienen
Boulder, CO	Boulder County Jail	Barbara Gigone[1]
Burlington, VT[3]	Chittenden Community Correctional Center	Philip Scripture[1]
Calhoun, GA	Gordon County Jail	Pat Baker
Canton, NY	St. Lawrence County Jail	Keith Knowlton
Colfax, WA	Whitman County Jail	Cleve Hunter
Colorado Springs, CO	El Paso County Jail	Harold Davis
Columbus, IN	Bartholomew County Jail	Michael McCoy
Concord, NH	Merrimack County House of Correction	William Potter[1]
Dothan, AL	Houston County Jail	A. B. Clark
Doylestown, PA	Bucks County Rehabilitation Center	Arthur Wallenstein[1]
Evansville, IN	Vanderburgh County Jail	James DeGroote
Fairfax, VA	Fairfax County Adult Detention Center	Wayne Huggins
Fort Collins, CO	Larimer County Detention Center	James Black

225

Location	Facility	Sheriff (1981)
Greely, CO	Weld County Jail	Harold Andrews
Hyannis, MA	Barnstable County Jail	John Bowes
Janesville, WI	Rock County Jail	Fred Falk
Lancaster, PA	Lancaster County Prison	Thomas Schlager[1]
LaPorte, IN	LaPorte County Jail	Jan Rose
Las Vegas, NV	Clark County Jail	Paul Bailey[1]
Lawrenceville, GA	Gwinnett County Jail	W. J. Dodd
Louisville, KY	Jefferson County Jail	Richard Frey[1]
Milwaukee, WI	Milwaukee County Detention Center	William Klamm
Milwaukee, WI	Milwaukee County House of Correction	Franklin Lotter[1]
Napa, CA	Napa County Jail	Brenda Hippard[1]
Newark, NJ	Essex County Jail	Albert Collier[1]
New Haven, CT[2]	New Haven Community Corrections Center	Victor Liburdi[1]
Orange, TX	Orange County Jail	E. L. Parker
Phoenix, AZ	Maricopa County Detention Center	P. L. Severson[1]
Pittsburgh, PA	Allegheny County Jail	James Jennings[1]
Port Washington, WI	Ozaukee County Jail	Fernando Perez
Raleigh, NC	Wake County Jail	John Baker
Richmond, VA	Henrico County Jail	James Turner
Salt Lake City, UT	Salt Lake County Jail	Peter Haywood
Schenectady, NY	Schenectady County Jail	Bernard Waldron
Sherman–Denison, TX	Grayson County Jail	Jack Driscoll
Shreveport, LA	Caddo Correctional Institute	Carl Hammonds[1]
Virginia Beach, VA	Virginia Beach City Jail	S. J. Smith

1. Chief administrator; the facility is not operated by a county sheriff.
2. The facilities in New Haven, Connecticut, and Burlington, Vermont, are the functional equivalents of local correctional centers, but cannot be technically described as jails because they are operated by state agencies. Burlington was included because the superintendent had sent representatives to an NIC training workshop in 1978, so it was one of the original 33 sites. New Haven was a supplemental site because of its status as an NIC area resource center and reputation for having high-quality inmate services.

References

Abramson, M. The criminalization of mentally disordered behavior: Possible side effects of a new mental health law. Hospital and Community Psychiatry, 23(4):101–105, 1972.

Advisory Commission on Intergovernmental Relations. *Jails: Intergovernmental Dimensions of a Local Problem.* Washington, DC: Author, 1983.

Aiken, M., & Hage, J. Organizational interdependence and intraorganizational structure. *American Sociological Review,* 33(6):912–930, 1968.

Aldrich, H. *Organizations and Environments.* Englewood Cliffs, NJ: Prentice-Hall, 1979.

American Association of Correctional Psychologists (AACP). Standards for psychology services in adult jails and prisons. *Criminal Justice and Behavior,* 7(1):81–127, 1980.

American Correctional Association (ACA). *Standards for Adult Local Detention Facilities* (2nd ed.). College Park, MD: Author, 1981.

American Medical Association (AMA). *Standards for Health Services in Jails* (2nd ed.). Chicago: Author, 1981.

American Public Health Association (APHA). *Standards for Health Services in Correctional Institutions.* Washington, DC: Author, 1976.

Anno, B., Hornung, C., & Lang, A. *An evaluation summary of the AMA's program to improve health care in jails (year three).* Paper presented at the Annual Meeting of the Academy of Criminal Justice Sciences, Philadelphia, 1981.

Arthur Bolton Associates. *A Study of the Need for and Availability of Mental Health Services for Mentally Disordered Jail Inmates and Juveniles in Detention Facilities.* Report prepared for the California Department of Health, Sacramento, 1976.

Attkisson, C., Hargreaves, W., Horowitz, M., & Soreson, J. *Evaluation of Human Service Programs.* New York: Academic Press, 1978.

Bachrach, L. L. Overview: Model programs for chronic mental patients. *American Journal of Psychiatry,* 137(9):1023–1031, 1980.

Bachrach, L. L. The homeless mentally ill and mental health services: An analytical review of the literature. In R. Lamb (ed.), *The Homeless Men-*

227

tally Ill: A Task Force Report of the American Psychiatric Association.
Washington, DC: American Psychiatric Association, 1984, pp. 11–54.

Bassuk, E., & Gerson, J. Deinstitutionalization and mental health services. *Scientific American, 238*(2):46–53, 1978.

Beigel, A., & H. Russell. Suicide attempts in jails: prognostic considerations. *Hospital and Community Psychiatry, 23*:361–362, 1972.

Bell v. Wolfish, 99 S.Ct. 1886 (1979).

Benson, J., Kunce, J., Thompson, C., & Allan, D. *Coordinating Human Services: A Sociological Study of an Interorganizational Network.* Columbia: University of Missouri Regional Rehabilitation Research Institute, 1973.

Blew, C., & P. Cirel. *Montgomery County Emergency Service.* Washington, DC: U.S. Government Printing Office, 1978.

Bogira, S. Psych team. *Chicago Reader,* April 10, 1981.

Bogue, D. J. *Skid Row in American Cities.* Chicago: Community and Family Study Center, University of Chicago, 1963.

Bowring v. Goodwin, 551 F. 2d. (3rd Cir. 1978).

Brodsky, S. Intervention models for mental health services in jails. In C. Dunn & H. J. Steadman (eds.), *Mental Health Services in Local Jails.* Washington, DC: U.S. Government Printing Service, 1982, pp. 126–148.

Buckman, S. Selected jail standards: A comparative survey. *Justice System Journal, 4*(1):100–113, 1978.

Bureau of Justice Statistics. *Jail Inmates, 1982.* Washington, DC: U.S. Government Printing Office, 1983.

Bureau of Justice Statistics. *Jail Inmates, 1986.* Washington, DC: U.S. Government Printing Office, 1987.

Carney, R. Overcrowding is blamed on the state. *Corrections Magazine, 8*(2):24–27, 1982.

Carrabba, C. Prisoners constitutional right to medical treatment: A right without substance? *New England Journal of Prison Law, 7*(2):341–377, 1981.

Charle, S. Suicide in the cellblocks—new programs attack the no. 1 killer of jail inmates. *Corrections Magazine, 7*(4):6–16, 1981.

Connors, K. The use of published minimum standards to determine when inadequate prison medical care constitutes cruel and unusual punishment. *Suffolk University Law Review, 13*:603–614, 1979.

Cormier, B. The practice of psychiatry in the prison society. *Bulletin of the American Academy of Psychiatry and Law, 1*(2):156–183, 1973.

Costonis, A. The mental health unit system: A critical evaluation and research statement. *Journal of Health and Human Behavior, 7*(2):75–83, 1966.

Culbertson, R. Personnel conflicts in jail management. *American Journal of Corrections, 39*(1):28–39, 1977.

Cumming, R., & Solway, H. The incarcerated psychiatrists. *Hospital and Community Psychiatry, 24*(9):631–632, 1973.

Danto, B. Perspectives and prescriptions. In B. Danto (ed.), *Jail House Blues.* Orchard Lake, MI: Epic, 1973, pp. 292–310.

Dunn, C., & Steadman, H. J. (eds.). *Mental Health Services in Local Jails* (DHHS Pub. No. ADM 82-1181). Washington, DC: U.S. Government Printing Office, 1982.

Estelle v. Gamble, 429 U.S. 97 (1976).

Farberow, N., & Shneidman, E. *The Cry for Help.* New York: McGraw-Hill, 1965.

Fairfax County, VA. *The Fairfax County Mobile Crisis Unit.* Unpublished report, Woodburn Center for Community Mental Health, Fairfax, VA, 1981.

Finney v. Arkansas Board of Corrections, 505 F. 2d. (8th Cir. 1974).

Flint, R. Standards: State of the art. In *The American Jail in Transition: Proceedings of the Second National Assembly on the Jail Crisis.* Washington, DC: U.S. Government Printing Office, 1978, pp. 32–39.

Florida Department of Health and Rehabilitative Services, Office of State Mental Health Programs. *Guidelines for Community Forensic Mental Health Programs.* Tallahassee: Author, 1984.

Ford, D., & Kerle, K. Jail standards—a different perspective. *Prison Journal, 61*(1)23–25, 1981.

Geller, J., & L. Lister. The process of criminal commitment for pretrial psychiatric examination: An evaluation. *American Journal of Psychiatry, 135*(1).53–63, 1978.

General Accounting Office (ed.). *Jail Inmates' Mental Health Care Neglected; State and Federal Attention Needed.* Washington, DC: U.S. Government Printing Office, 1980.

Goldfarb, R. *Jails.* Garden City, NY: Anchor Books, 1976.

Goldkamp, J. *Inmates of American Jails: A Descriptive Study.* Albany, NY: Criminal Justice Research Center, 1978.

Goldmeier, J., Sauer, R., & White, V. A halfway house for mentally ill offenders. *American Journal of Psychiatry, 134*(1):45–49, 1977.

Guy, E., Platt, J. J., Zwerling, J., & Bullock, S. Mental health status of prisoners in an urban jail. *Criminal Justice and Behavior, 12*(1):29–53, 1985.

Haley, M. Developing a program of mental health services in a rural county jail. *Hospital and Community Psychiatry, 31*(9):631–632, 1980.

Hall, R. *Organizations, Structure and Process* (3rd ed.). Englewood Cliffs, NJ: Prentice-Hall, 1982.

Hall, R., Clark, J., & Giordano, P. *The Extent and Correlates of Interorganizational Conflict.* Unpublished report, Department of Sociology, State University of New York at Albany, 1978.

Harding, J., & McPheeters, H. Distribution of mental health professionals in the South: A research project. *Hospital and Community Psychiatry, 30*(11):772–775, 1979.

Harris, M., & Spiller, D. *After Decision: Implementation of Judicial Decrees in Correctional Settings*. Washington, DC: National Institute of Law Enforcement and Criminal Justice, 1977.

Harvard Law Review. Mental health litigation: Implementing institutional reform. *Mental Disability Law Reporter, 2*(2-3):221-233, 1977.

Hasenfeld, Y. People processing organizations: An exchange approach. *American Sociological Review, 37*(3):256-263, 1972.

Henderson, T. *Strategies for Implementing Standards/Inspection Programs*. Alexandria, VA: Institute of Economic and Policy Studies, 1981.

Hopper, K., Baxter, E., & Cox, S. Not making it crazy: The young homeless patients in New York City. *New Directions in Mental Health Services*, No. 14:33-42, 1982.

Inmates v. Pierce, 489 F. Supp. 638 (1980).

Isolation cells for mentally ill criticized. *Milwaukee Journal*, June 4, 1980, p. 5.

Janovsky, A., Scallet, L., & Jaskulski, T. *The County Government Role in Mental Health Systems*. Washington, DC: National Association of Counties Research, 1982.

Jones v. Wittenberg, 330 F. Supp. 707, W.D. Ohio (1971).

Kaufman, E. Can comprehensive mental health care be provided in an overcrowded prison system? *Journal of Psychiatry and the Law, 1*(2):243-262, 1973.

Kerle, K., & Ford, F. *The State of Our Nation's Jails, 1982*. Washington, DC: National Sheriff's Association, 1982.

Kirk, R., & Spears, R. Development of rural health services. *Medical Care, 17*(2):175-181, 1979.

Lamb, H. R. The new asylum in the community. *Archives of General Psychiatry, 36*:129-134, 1979.

Lamb, H. R., & Grant, R. The mentally ill in an urban county jail. *Archives of General Psychiatry, 39*(1):17-22, 1982.

Leaf, P. Alabama after *Wyatt*: PIL intervention into a mental health services delivery system. In B. Weissbrod, J. Handler, & N. Lomesat, (eds.), *Public Interest Law: An Economic and Institutional Analysis*. Berkeley: University of California Press, 1978, pp. 374-393.

Leaf, P. and Holt, M. How *Wyatt* affected patients. In L. Jones & R. Parlour (eds.) Wyatt v. Stickney: *Retrospect and Prospect*. New York: Grune & Stratton, 1981, pp. 49-109.

Lehman, E. *Coordinating Health Care: Explorations in Interorganizational Relations*. Beverly Hills, CA: Sage, 1975.

Lunden, W. *The Prison Warden and the Custodial Staff*. Springfield, IL: Charles C Thomas, 1965.

Massachusetts Special Commission to Investigate Suicides in Municipal Detention Centers. *Suicides in Massachusetts Lockups, 1973-1984*. Boston: Author, 1984.

Meloy, J. R. Inpatient psychiatric treatment in a county jail. *Journal of Psychiatry and the Law, 13*(3-4):373-396, 1985.

Miller, E. *Jail Management*. Lexington, MA: Lexington Books, 1978.

Monahan, J., & McDonough, L. B. Delivering community mental health services to a county jail population: A research note. *Bulletin of the American Academy of Psychiatry and the Law*, 8(1)28-32, 1980.

Monahan, J., & Steadman, H. Crime and mental disorder: An epidemiological approach. In N. Morris & M. Towrey (eds.), *Annual Review of Crime and Justice* (Vol. 4). Chicago: University of Chicago Press, 1982, pp. 145-189.

Morgan, C. *The Special National Workshop on Mental Health Services in Jails*. Baltimore: National Institute of Corrections, 1978.

Morgan C. Developing mental health services for local jails. *Criminal Justice and Behavior*, 8(3):250-274, 1981.

Morrissey, J. Deinstitutionalizing the mentally ill: Processes, outcomes and new directions. In W. Gove (ed.), *Deviance and Mental Illness*. Beverly Hills, CA: Sage, 1982a, pp. 147-176.

Morrissey, J. Assessing interorganizational linkages: Towards a systems analysis of community support programs at the local level. In R. Tessler & H. Goldman (eds.), *The Chronically Mentally Ill: Assessing Community Support Programs*. Cambridge, MA: Ballinger, 1982b, pp. 159-191

Morrissey, J., Steadman, H., & Kilburn, H. Organizational issues in the delivery of jail mental health services. In J. Greenley (ed.), *Research in Community and Mental Health* (Vol. 3). Greenwich, CT: JAI Press, 1983, pp. 291-317.

Morrissey, J., & Tessler, R. Selection processes in state mental hospitalization: Policy issues and research directions. In M. Lewis (ed.), *Social Problems and Public Policy. A Research Annual* (Vol. 2). Greenwich, CT: JAI Press, 1982, pp 35-79.

National Advisory Commission on Criminal Justice Standards and Goals. Standards and goals for local correctional facilities. In P. Cromwell (ed.), *Jails and Justice*. Englewood Cliffs, NJ: Prentice-Hall 1975, pp. 252-266.

National Association of Counties. National notes. *Pretrial Reporter*, 7(6):3-12, 1982.

National Coalition for Jail Reform. *Jail—The New Mental Institution*. Washington, DC: Author, undated.

National Center on Institutions and Alternatives. *And Darkness Closes in . . . National Study of Jail Suicides*. Alexandria, VA: Author, 1981.

Neugebauer, R., Dohrenwend, B., & Dohrenwend, B. Formulation of hypotheses about the true prevalence of functional psychiatric disorders among adults in the United States. In B. Dohrenwend, B. Dohrenwend, M. Gould, B. Link, R. Neugebauer, & R. Wunsch-Hitzig (eds.), *Mental Illness in the United States: Epidemiological Estimates*. New York: Praeger, 1980.

New Jails: Boom for builders, bust for budgets. *Business Week*, February 9, 1981, pp. 74-80.

New York State Commission on Correction, Medical Review Board. *Memo on Suicides in Correctional Facilities in 1983 and 1984.* Albany, NY: Author, 1985.

New York State Commission on Corrections & New York State Office of Mental Health: *New York State local forensic suicide crisis service model: Policy and procedure manual for mental health programs.* Utica, IL: Utica Press, 1986.

Newman, C., & Price, B. Jails and services for inmates: A perspective on some critical issues. *Criminology, 14*(4):501–502, 1977a.

Newman, C., & Price B. *Jails and Drug Treatment.* Beverly Hills, CA: Sage, 1977b.

Nielsen, E. Community mental health services in the community jail. *Community Mental Health Journal, 15*(1):27–32, 1979.

O'Keefe, J. *Department of Mental Health Correctional Study.* Report prepared for the Massachusetts Department of Mental Health, Boston, 1980.

O'Neil, J. Standards: State of the art. In *The American Jail in Transition: Proceedings of the Second National Assembly on the Jail Crisis.* Washington, DC: U.S. Government Printing Office, 1978, pp. 34–35.

Parsons, T. The mental hospital as a type of organization. In M. Greenblatt, D. J. Levinson, & R. H. Williams (eds.), *The Patient and the Mental Hospital.* Glencoe, IL: Free Press, 1957, pp. 108–129.

Perrow, C. Hospitals: Technology, structure and goals. In J. March (ed.), *Handbook of Organizations.* Chicago: Rand McNally, 1965, pp. 910–971.

Perrow, C. Reality adjustment: A young institution settles for humane care. *Social Problems, 14*(1):69–79, 1966.

Perrow, C. *Organizational Analysis: A Sociological View.* Monterey, CA: Brooks/Cole, 1970.

Petrich, J. Psychiatric treatment in jail: An experiment in health care delivery. *Hospital and Community Psychiatry, 27*(6):413–415, 1976.

Pondy, L. Varieties of organizational conflict. *Administrative Science Quarterly, 14*(4):498–505, 1969.

Powelson, H., & Bendix, R. Psychiatry in prison. *Psychiatry, 14*(1):73–86, 1951.

Prestholdt, P., Lane, I., & Matthews, C. Predicting staff nurse turnover. *Nursing Outlook, 36* (May–June): 145–147, 1988.

Price, J. *The Study of Turnover.* Ames: Iowa State University Press, 1977.

Rawls, W. Crises and cutbacks stirring fresh concern on state of the nation's prisons. *New York Times,* January 5, 1982a, p. A-9.

Rawls, W. Judges' authority in prison reform attacked. *New York Times,* May 18, 1982b, p. A-21.

Ringel, N. B., & Segal, A. C. A mental health center's influence in a county jail. *Journal of Community Psychology, 14*: 171–182, 1986.

Robitscher, J. Moving patients out of hospitals—in whose interest? In P. Ahmed & S. Plog (eds.) *State Mental Hospitals: What Happens When They Close.* New York: Plenum, 1976, pp. 141–176.

Rooney, K. Response of the Department of Justice. In U.S. General Accounting Office (ed.), *Jail Inmates' Mental Health Care Neglected; State and Federal Attention Needed.* Washington, DC: U.S. Government Printing Office, 1980, pp. 70–74.

Roth, L. Correctional psychiatry. In W. Curran, A. McGarry, & C. Retty (eds.), *Modern Legal Medicine, Psychiatry and Forensic Science.* Philadelphia: F. A. Davis, 1980, pp. 667–719.

Russel, W. Mentally ill and in jail. *Advance, 14*(1):43, 1980.

Sandall, H., Hawley, T. T., & Gordon, G. C. The St. Louis community homes program: Graduated support for long-term care. *American Journal of Psychiatry, 132*:617–622, 1975.

Schermerhorn, J. Determinants of interorganizational cooperation. *Academy of Management Journal, 18*(6):846–856, 1975.

Schleifer, C., & Derbyshire, R. Clinical change in jail-referred mental patients. *Archives of General Psychiatry, 18*(1):42–46, 1968.

Schuckit, M., Herrman, G., & Schuckit, J. The importance of psychiatric illness in newly arrested prisoners. *Journal of Nervous and Mental Disease, 165*(2):118–125, 1977.

Scull, A. *Decarceration: Community Treatment and the Deviant—A Radical View.* Englewood Cliffs, NJ: Prentice-Hall, 1977.

Singer, R. Providing mental health services for jail inmates: Legal perspectives. *Journal of Prison Health, 1*(2):105–129, 1981.

Steadman, H., Cocozza, J., & Lee, S. From maximum security to secure treatment: Organizational constraints. *Human Organization, 37*(3):276–284, 1978.

Steadman, H., & Ribner, S. Changing perceptions of the mental health needs of inmates in local jails. *American Journal of Psychiatry, 137*(9):1115–1116, 1980.

Steinwald, C. *Medical Care in U.S. Jails: A 1972 AMA Survey.* Chicago: American Medical Association, Center for Health Services Research and Development, 1973.

Street, D., Vinter, R., & Perrow, C. *Organization for Treatment.* New York: Free Press, 1966.

Swank, G., & Winer, D. Occurrence of psychiatric disorder in a county jail population. *American Journal of Psychiatry, 133*(11):1331–1333, 1976.

Talbott, J. E. *Unified mental health systems: Utopia unrealized.* San Francisco: Jossey-Bass, 1983.

Tessler, R., & Goldman, H. (eds.). *The Chronically Mentally Ill: Assessing Community Support Programs.* Cambridge, MA: Ballinger, 1982.

Thirty six percent of guards not trained, new jail chief says. *Pittsburgh Press,* August 6, 1980, p. A-16.

Thompson, J., & W. McEwen. Organizational goals and environment: Goal setting as an interaction process. *American Sociological Review, 23*(February):23–31, 1958.

Tierney, T. R., & Wright, N. Minimizing turnover problem: A behavioral approach. *Supervisor Nurse, 4* (August): 47–57, 1933.

Turner, J., & TenHoor, W. NIMH Community Support Program: Pilto approach to a needed social reform. *Schizophrenia Bulletin, 4*:319–344, 1978.

U.S. Children's Bureau. *Child Welfare Statistics, 1964.* Washington, DC: U.S. Government Printing Office, 1965.

U.S. Department of Health and Human Services. *Toward a National Plan for the Chronically Mentally Ill.* Washington, DC: U.S. Government Printing Office, 1980.

U.S. Department of Justice. *Profile of Jail Inmates: Sociodemographic Findings from the 1978 Survey of Inmates of Local Jails.* Washington, DC: U.S. Government Printing Office, 1980a.

U.S. Department of Justice. *Federal Standards for Prisons and Jails.* Washington, DC: U.S. Government Printing Office, 1980b.

U.S. Department of Justice. *Census of Jails, 1978.* Washington, DC: U.S. Government Printing Office, 1981.

Van de Ven, A., & Ferry, D. *Measuring and Assessing Organizations.* New York: Wiley, 1980.

Van Patten, R., & Spar, J. E. The board and care home: Does it deserve a bad press? *Hospital and Community Psychiatry, 30*:461–464, 1979.

Warner, R. *Recovery from Schizophrenia: Psychiatry and Political Economy.* Boston: Routledge & Kegan Paul, 1985.

Warren, R. The interorganizational field as a focus for investigation. *Administrative Science Quarterly, 12*(December):396–419, 1967.

Warren, R., Bergunder, A., & Rose, S. *The Structure of Urban Reform.* Lexington, MA: D.C. Heath, 1974.

Weiner, R. Managing the interorganizational environment in corrections. *Federal Probation, 44*(4):16–19, 1980.

Whetten, D. Toward a contingency model for designing interorganizational service delivery systems. *Organization and Administrative Sciences, 8*(2):77–96, 1977.

Whitmer, G. From hospitals to jails: The fate of California's deinstitutionalized mentally ill. *American Journal of Orthopsychiatry, 50*(1):65–75, 1980.

Wilson, R. Who will care for the mad and bad? *Corrections Magazine, 6*(1):5–17, 1980.

Winner, E. An Introduction to the constitutional law of prison medical care. *Journal of Prison Health, 1*(1):67–84, 1981.

Zald, M. Comparative analysis and measurement of organizational goals: The case of correctional institutions for delinquents. *Sociological Quarterly, 4*(3):206–230, 1963.

Zitrin, A., Hardesty, A., & Burdock, E. Crime and violence among mental patients. *American Journal of Psychiatry, 133*(2):142–149, 1976.

Index